LOCAL COLOUR

TRAVELS IN THE OTHER AUSTRALIA

PHOTOGRAPHY AND TEXT BY BILL BACHMAN

ADDITIONAL TEXT BY TIM WINTON

LOCAL COLOUR

Published by Local Colour Limited
Ground Floor, 2 Lower Kai Yuen Lane
North Point, Hong Kong
Tel (852) 2590 0733 Fax (852) 2590 0433
ppro@netvigator.com

First Australian edition published 1994
Revised edition published 1998

A CIP catalogue record for this is available from the British Library.

ISBN 962-217-546-5

Editor: John Ross
Design: David Hughes, Philip Choi
Map design: David Hughes

Printed and bound in Hong Kong

In loving memory of John and Margaret Baker

ENDPAPERS: A surrealistic swirl of tiger eye and jasper found near the Western Australian mining town of Meekatharra reveals local colour in its purist form.
Tiger eye is created when quartz replaces the fibres in asbestos, producing shimmering bands of colour.

TITLE PAGE: Sea and sky meet in layers of azure off Eighty Mile Beach at Wallal Downs Station, on the northwest coast of Western Australia.

To Sally, for all the miles
and the memories.
This is your book, too.

CONTENTS

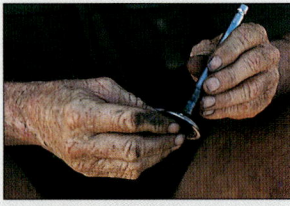

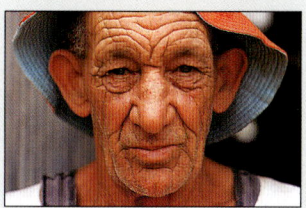

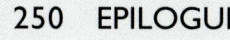

INTRODUCTION

RICK BERTRAM • ROY HILL, WA

I have found in the faces of strangers in places
that most of us never do more than pass through,
a love of this land that can make such demands
on the heart and yet somehow can leave you renewed

We live on the edge of this land we call home,
we worship the water — yet somehow we know
that deep in the heartland where all of us dwell
lie the reasons we're Aussies it ain't hard to tell

MIKE McCLELLAN, *The Heartland* (1989)

GANTHEAUME POINT • BROOME. WA

Just before sundown one day in May 1991 I was prowling around the back streets of Coober Pedy, when I met an opal miner named Gary. We stood talking by his front fence, which was made of mismatched panels of corrugated iron jammed into the ground. Covering the bare earth between the fence and his front door was possibly the world's largest collection of Holden motorcar wheels, neatly organised in rows according to year and model. Here, I thought, was a man with a truly vernacular approach to garden design.

Gary told me he'd once lived "down South," but had left both a wife and the city behind in 1983. Over the next four years (spent contemplatively swinging a pick down a mineshaft) he rethought his life, and in due course became a born-again Christian and "turned all his enemies to friends," whatever that was supposed to mean. By his own account, he now lived a happy life with a cat, a dog and a boarder in a home-made dugout just in front of Ice Cream Hill.

Our conversation eventually turned to travel, and one of the things he said stuck in my mind: "So much of Australia remains undiscovered, you know. In fact, most Australians have no idea what their country is really like. But it's different out here. You can't live all your life in the Southeast and really call yourself an Australian."

ROSS THOMPSON AND "CHUCK" • BROOMEHILL, WA

BLUE HEELER HOTEL • KYNUNA, WESTERN QLD

DERBY RACES • WEST KIMBERLEY, WA   SHEARERS' CAMP • SHARK BAY, WA   FENCE NEAR COPLEY, SA

Most Australians do just that, however. Despite an historical penchant for exploration and settlement and a national mythology rooted in the vast, untracked Outback, fewer than five million people live in rural Australia today, and the numbers are continually shrinking. More than 80 percent of the population lives in six modern coastal cities and their hinterland, gazing outward and sharing a hybrid culture that is predominantly Anglo-American, blended with numerous other imported flavours.

Though Australia's cities have always quite logically been at the national epicentre, entire volumes have also been devoted to exploring Gary's thesis that the genuine Australia lies inland, far from the multicultural melting pot. It was after all the rugged, arid heartland that gave rise to the archetypal white Australian, the bushman. Celebrated in legend and song for his courage, strength, sense of equality and unaffected good humour, "the man from out back" was for several generations the role model for an entire race of people, and along with the vast spaces surrounding him, came to epitomise all that was uniquely Australian.

These days, the mountain range on the horizon has well and truly been replaced by the back fence, and it can quite easily be argued that the beach and the Sunday barbecue are the heart and soul of the modern Australian ethos. Nevertheless, the bush still looms large in the collective imagination, and is visited by increasing numbers of travellers every year, many bent on discovering "the real Australia." In truth, of course, the vital essences of Australia are found everywhere from Ayers Rock to the suburban corner shop, but my opal-mining friend Gary definitely had a point: the physical heartland *is* different. Even if most of us admire it from a distance, we still depend on it as the source of many of the country's most potent traditions and values, and it remains an important cultural breeding ground.

BARNEY ROSE • TANAMI DOWNS, NT   COMMUNITY CENTRE • BYRON BAY, NSW

JOE GILMOUR, STARDUST AMUSEMENTS • LAJAMANU, NT

I first ventured inland in 1987, on a seven-month voyage of discovery that opened my eyes to the wonders of outback Australia and whetted my appetite for further exploration. When I set off again in mid-1990 on a much longer odyssey, it was with a book like this in mind. In the beginning I had no specific theme to guide me, and as I travelled the focus of the project had a habit of shifting all over the place. I went through landscape phases and portrait phases, literal phases and abstract phases. From time to time I'd become obsessed with rocks and trees, or weird signs and roadside wrecks - all dissociated bits and pieces of Australia, linked only by my own tyre tracks and footprints. Basically, I just kept patiently exploring in the hope that a unifying theme would eventually emerge.

Somewhere around the halfway point of my travels, in line with Gary's "It's another country out there" credo, I began to think of the outback as "The Other Australia," which helped to give some common focus to my work, but it wasn't until my last night on the road, more than 18 months after I left Melbourne, that the actual title of this book came to me. I was standing under the shower in a caravan park in Echuca, Victoria, and all of a sudden there it was: "Local Colour."

It's funny how the simplest things can take such a long time to evolve. What I had finally come to realise is that the random scraps of landscape and lifestyle that I'd been photographing *were* the theme. All along I'd been creating one big picture out of many small ones, like the scavenged, variegated pieces of tin that made up Gary's fence.

Afterward, for a while I worried that this collage might become caricature, but ultimately I also realised that cataloguing the sometimes-odd realities of the bush is not a matter of glamourising, lampooning, or waxing nostalgic over the outback way of life, but simply of acknowledging the abundance of local colour that decorates our heartland. By doing so, we celebrate many of the things that make us what we are.

BILL BACHMAN
Melbourne, June 1994

SPRING WILDFLOWERS • EAST PILBARA, WA

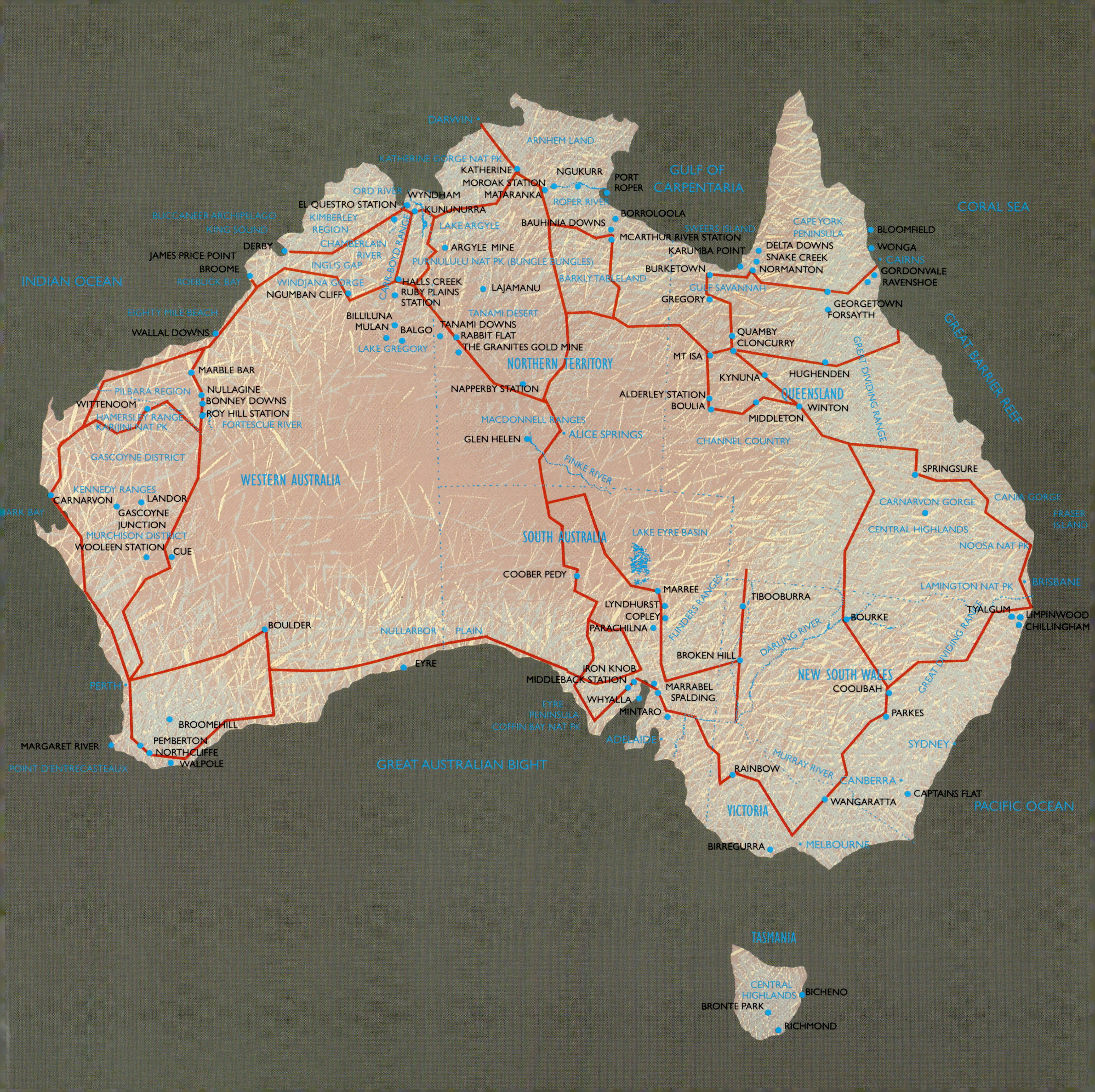

DARWIN
ARNHEM LAND
KATHERINE GORGE NAT PK
KATHERINE
NGUKURR
MOROAK STATION
MATARANKA
PORT ROPER
GULF OF CARPENTARIA
ROPER RIVER
ORD RIVER
WYNDHAM
EL QUESTRO STATION
KUNUNURRA
BUCCANEER ARCHIPELAGO
KIMBERLEY REGION
KING SOUND
LAKE ARGYLE
BORROLOOLA
BAUHINIA DOWNS
CORAL SEA
CAPE YORK PENINSULA
SWEERS ISLAND
BLOOMFIELD
MCARTHUR RIVER STATION
DERBY
CHAMBERLAIN RIVER
ARGYLE MINE
DELTA DOWNS
WONGA
JAMES PRICE POINT
CARR BOYD RANGE
KARUMBA POINT
SNAKE CREEK
CAIRNS
BROOME
INGLIS GAP
PURNULULU NAT PK (BUNGLE BUNGLES)
BURKETOWN
NORMANTON
GORDONVALE
INDIAN OCEAN
ROEBUCK BAY
WINDJANA GORGE
HALLS CREEK
BARKLY TABLELAND
RAVENSHOE
NGUMBAN CLIFF
RUBY PLAINS STATION
LAJAMANU
GULF SAVANNAH
GREGORY
GEORGETOWN
EIGHTY MILE BEACH
FORSAYTH
BILLILUNA
TANAMI DESERT
MULAN
TANAMI DOWNS
BALGO
GREAT BARRIER REEF
WALLAL DOWNS
RABBIT FLAT
QUAMBY
LAKE GREGORY
THE GRANITES GOLD MINE
CLONCURRY
MT ISA
NORTHERN TERRITORY
HUGHENDEN
MARBLE BAR
KYNUNA
GREAT DIVIDING RANGE
PILBARA REGION
NULLAGINE
NAPPERBY STATION
QUEENSLAND
WITTENOOM
BONNEY DOWNS
ALDERLEY STATION
BOULIA
WINTON
HAMERSLEY RANGE
ROY HILL STATION
KARIJINI NAT PK
FORTESCUE RIVER
MACDONNELL RANGES
MIDDLETON
ALICE SPRINGS
CHANNEL COUNTRY
GLEN HELEN
GASCOYNE DISTRICT
SPRINGSURE
FINKE RIVER
WESTERN AUSTRALIA
KENNEDY RANGES
CANIA GORGE
CARNARVON
LANDOR
CARNARVON GORGE
SHARK BAY
GASCOYNE JUNCTION
FRASER ISLAND
CENTRAL HIGHLANDS
MURCHISON DISTRICT
LAKE EYRE BASIN
SOUTH AUSTRALIA
WOOLEEN STATION
CUE
NOOSA NAT PK
COOBER PEDY
BRISBANE
MARREE
LAMINGTON NAT PK
FLINDERS RANGES
TIBOOBURRA
LYNDHURST
TYALGUM
LIMPINWOOD
COPLEY
BOURKE
CHILLINGHAM
BOULDER
PARACHILNA
NULLARBOR PLAIN
DARLING RIVER
BROKEN HILL
IRON KNOB
NEW SOUTH WALES
EYRE
PERTH
MIDDLEBACK STATION
COOLIBAH
MARRABEL
WHYALLA
SPALDING
GREAT DIVIDING RANGE
EYRE PENINSULA
MINTARO
PARKES
BROOMEHILL
COFFIN BAY NAT PK
MARGARET RIVER
PEMBERTON
ADELAIDE
SYDNEY
NORTHCLIFFE
WALPOLE
GREAT AUSTRALIAN BIGHT
MURRAY RIVER
POINT D'ENTRECASTEAUX
RAINBOW
CANBERRA
CAPTAINS FLAT
WANGARATTA
PACIFIC OCEAN
VICTORIA
BIRREGURRA
MELBOURNE
TASMANIA
CENTRAL HIGHLANDS
BICHENO
BRONTE PARK
RICHMOND

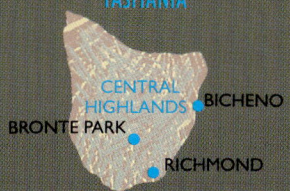

LOCAL COLOUR

The Australian bush has no monopoly on local colour. There are no fewer sights to be seen in the cities, no fewer characters to be stumbled upon, no less peculiarity, no dearth of colours and textures. Indeed, the eye feasts wherever it travels. But local colour is strongest and most memorable, I think, when it is most hard-won. Hard-won in the sense of developing in isolation, under duress, and hard-won for the viewer, when the drive has been a bone-shaker, the day longer than it had any right to be, and the sight of something unique most welcome.

The natural pigments of the outback (taking local colour most literally for a moment) are all the more intense and sobering because of their solitude. Out there you have the sense of things having worn, percolated, crystallized and settled into shape over great time and with vast mystery. The weird span of rock impossibly upright against the sky. The glowing sentinels of termite mounds eerily taking up position on the plain, their throbbing colour almost unnatural. The sudden appearance against the late afternoon sky of that most earthbound of trees, the boab, with its glutton belly and empty arms. All seem so complete in such an unfinished-looking landscape. Perhaps it is both isolation and silence that cause things there to be seen so vividly. Distance produces a fasting effect, and a visual event shocks the senses like the first glass of wine in a year. Coming upon such sights in the taciturn interior imparts a sense of gravity. You stare and grunt; you don't

UNFINISHED MURAL ON WALL OF ABORIGINAL ART CENTRE • ALICE SPRINGS, NT

bother to make comparisons, for the strongest sense of place comes when a gully, a river, a tree, a meeting of mineral veins simply insists on itself, makes itself instantly exclusive. Long before the postcards and hype, places like Uluru and the Bungles became iconic images from their very strength of character and their sense of being one-off creations. This same particularity carries to the small things, the tiny icons out there that await the traveller, the worker, the watcher, like a sudden willy-willy twisting across the dust, the stupendous sunset that lacks an artistic education, the unrepeatable things like the movement of light, of dust, of water. Little events, small mercies in a landscape that never gives an inch and is immune to romantic sentiment. Again, this is not unique to the outback, but more able to be seen here, less likely to be lost in the blur of competing activity, in the million moments the eye can't process in a melee.

As with landscape, humans are most striking in isolation; people are so often more memorable for having been left alone. Australia's outback people are spread so thinly across the continent that, like signposts, turn-offs, natural wonders, they become events in themselves. They are most colourful when they are unselfconscious or simply enjoying the idea of themselves, for people who are at ease with how they are and where they are and what they do are able to allow themselves to be seen. It's not just that they're docile photographic or conversational subjects who'll shrug and let you photograph them or question them with their hat cocked back and their boot on the rail, but that they are self-possessed and straight-forward enough to let themselves be known. What you see is pretty much what you get. They see this as being "down to earth" and a virtue, and they're surely right to think so. Strength of character and strength of place go together, here where neurosis is an illness and not a pastime.

In a more theatrical sense, perhaps, isolation also produces the bizarre and hilarious, not always from the madness of the desert or the mangrove, or an excess of beer and rum (though these are often sources of inspiration out where the traffic signals are weak and the TV signal worse) but from the dire need to entertain yourself and others. That's where much of Outback Gothic springs from.

A publican in northwest Queensland will have a galah that picks his teeth for him, another in Tasmania will keep a "watchpig," complete with studded collar, to ward off burglars. Someone in Wyndham will paint a dead tree green just for the hell of it, while others will spend hours inscribing signs with daggy puns and old jokes that raise a laugh for the simple fact that someone has bothered. Bizarre entertainments spring up. A racing carnival will occur in the middle of nowhere. Men will race mudcrabs at Snake Creek and camels in Alice Springs, kids will race goats behind a pub in western New South Wales. Out by the killing shed on a quiet station, a pair of five-year-olds will sail gum leaves down a gutter of blood still steaming from a slaughtered beast.

Small entertainments, little splashes of brightness. Local colour of the most arresting kind always breeds and brews in the slow lane. It isn't the driven and desperate eccentricity of the inner city, where the need to shock and be noticed is more vital; it's the particularity that comes from tidal pace, meteorological pace, seasonal pace, in a zone where lifestyle comes before livelihood, where politics are extremely conservative and personalities most liberal indeed.

Famous sights, famous places, famous people always end up imitating themselves. But there are plenty of small, unknown, un-named substitutes for them. No doubt there are pubs all over the interior and the tropics where the locals have gingered up the act for the tourists and the photographers and writers, but we've yet to see local colour become a commodity (and therefore merely a memory) altogether. And if the locals do ham it up? Well, they know how vicariously the suburban Australian lives through them, so perhaps they're entitled. After all, they are the guardians of the national idea.

Why would anybody turn a watertank into a huge replica of a can of Foster's? Some leftover paint lying around? A bit of time heavy on the hands? For the sake of conversation at the boundary gate, or to have it in the local rag and thereby achieve some kind of immortality? All the usual cultural and artistic imponderables apply, I'm sure. Why name your house, build a wall of beer bottles in the pattern of the national flag, fill your garden with gnomes, paint a landscape on a supermarket wall? The best answer is always a grin and a shrug, and it's the one most often given.

Local colour comes from a land and a people making themselves up as they go along, hardly noticing their great distinction, not minding if anybody else does, and shrugging it off lightly, with amusement and some doubt.

TIM WINTON

MANGROVE AT HIGH TIDE · ROEBUCK BAY, WEST KIMBERLEY, WA

A lone mangrove just manages to keep its head above the aquamarine waters of the Indian Ocean near Broome.
Low tide will find it high and dry, with mudflats extending nearly to the horizon.

RAY KENNEDY, FORTESCUE RIVER • ROY HILL STATION, EAST PILBARA, WA

The rusty waters of a landlocked waterhole in the Pilbara colour-coordinate with the grimy sweatband on grazier Ray Kennedy's hat.

WATERTANK, QUAMBY HOTEL • GULF REGION, NORTHWEST QLD

Matched temporarily (nothing keeps its gloss for long under Australia's tropical sun) by the rich pigments of earth and sky, this bright bit of folk art is as good as flashing neon to thirsty travellers on the road from Cloncurry to the Carpentaria coast of Queensland.

(RIGHT) TERMITE MOUNDS NEAR FIDDLERS LAKE • TANAMI DESERT, NT

Crimson castles inhabited by tens of thousands – sometimes millions – of termites, these mounds are widespread across Australia's dry inland, sometimes hundreds to the hectare. Beneath each impregnable and perfectly humidified mound is an extensive gallery of tunnels running deep underground and radiating outward toward the spinifex hummocks that provide nourishment.

MUDSTONE FORMATION, EDOLINE ISLAND
BUCCANEER ARCHIPELAGO
NW KIMBERLEY COAST, WA

The eccentric geology of Australia is typified
by this frozen flag of crumbling mudstone on
one of the more than 800 islands that guard
the entrance to King Sound, north of Derby.
Mostly dry and rocky, these islands, rather like
flung handfuls of gravel, occupy waters that
remain largely uncharted since first explored
by Captain Phillip Parker King during his
circumnavigation of Australia in the 1820s.

COASTAL SANDSTONE
ROEBUCK BAY NEAR BROOME, WA

Surreal sandstone merges with the azure
blue of sea and sky on the west Kimberley
coast. These shallow waters, which become
vast mudflats at low tide, are vital feeding
grounds for huge numbers – over 170,000
have been counted on a single occasion –
of migratory wading birds on their way
from Siberia and other northern habitats
to the southern shores of Australia.

SNAPPY GUMS AND TERMITE MOUNDS • WEANO GORGE, KARIJINI NAT PK, WA

The vivid primary colours of the Pilbara had their origin two and a half billion years ago, when the ironstone ranges of the Hamersley Basin were the bed of a rust-red sea. There is a widely-held scientific belief that, through a complex series of chemical and biological events, these same waters gave rise to the chlorophyll molecule, which itself is directly responsible for the blue sky and green foliage in our modern landscapes. The red earthtones in this photograph come from the oxidized sediments left behind by the retreating ocean; more than two km thick in places, what was once mere silt is now one of the richest deposits of iron ore in the world.

BOAB GROVE NEAR DERBY • WEST KIMBERLEY, WA

Filigreed against a surreal Kimberley sunset, these boabs are closely related to Africa's giant baobabs. Both species are highly adapted to drought, and their similarities suggest a common ancestor in Gondwanaland, the mega-continent that many scientists think once embraced Australia, Africa, Antarctica, South America and the Indian subcontinent.

ROCK OUTCROP AND SPINIFEX • NE PILBARA NEAR MARBLE BAR, WA

Like a burrowing echidna, a spiky outcrop bristles with spinifex on a rocky plain near Marble Bar. Spinifex thrives on poor soils, comes in 30 different species, and covers 22 percent of the Australian continent. Rock comes in innumerable species, and is found just about everywhere.

CLAYSTONE AND CONVOLVULUS VINE • JAMES PRICE POINT, WEST KIMBERLEY, WA

A sociable climber hugs a low coastal cliff along the Dampier Peninsula, north of Broome.

EL QUESTRO GORGE • EAST KIMBERLEY, WA

A grazier's Garden of Eden, El Questro Gorge takes its name from the million-acre cattle station on which it is located, about 100 km west of Kununurra. The Kimberley region contains a great diversity of species and habitats, including scattered pockets of tropical rainforest. Unlike classical "jungles" of the wet tropics, they are distinguished by green canopies, and contain a profusion of rainforest plants and vines. The canopy creates a "greenhouse effect" that maintains humidity throughout the long winter dry season.

SMOKO, ARGYLE DIAMOND MINE
EAST KIMBERLEY, WA

Balanced on the toes of a giant, workers
in the main ore pit take morning tea in the
bucket of a hydraulic excavator. Argyle
operates three such machines. Each costs
$6.5 million, weighs 450 tonnes, and can
lift 19 cubic metres (about 45 tonnes) in a
single shovelful. More than 175 million
tonnes of ore, yielding over 45 tonnes of
diamonds, were taken from the main pit
between 1986, when the mine opened,
and the end of 1992.

GRADER AND BOAB TREE • ARGYLE DIAMOND MINE, EAST KIMBERLEY, WA

Anchored firmly to the earth that is being stripped from around it, this outback ancient looks on impassively
while miners struggle to extract diamonds from the dust of Smoke Creek, 2200 kilometres northeast of Perth.
Geologists first found diamonds here in 1979; today, the Argyle mine is the world's biggest producer.

SWIMMERS AT FORTESCUE FALLS • KARIJINI (HAMERSLEY RANGES) NAT PK, WA

Deep permanent pools at the base of steep-walled gorges contain the lifeblood of the Pilbara's dry ironstone ranges.
Despite a torrid climate, the water remains cold year-round because the sun reaches into the canyons for only a few hours every day.

NOEL FULLERTON ABOARD "MALACHI"
RAINBOW VALLEY, NT

In the Northern Territory, the name Fullerton is synonymous with camels. Owner of the Virginia Camel Farm, 90 km south of Alice Springs, Noel Fullerton is probably Australia's best-known camel breeder and safari operator, and founded the Camel Cup, now an important annual fixture on the Alice Springs racing calendar.

Camels were first introduced to Australia by Afghans around 1860, and played a very important role in opening up the interior. For more than 50 years until the 1920s, camel trains of up to 70 animals radiated into the outback from railheads and ports. Today, more than 40,000 of their descendants roam unmolested through large areas of inland Australia. They form one of the purest herds in the world, and are much sought after as bloodstock by Middle Eastern buyers.

JACK BLACK AND AUB CROMPTON • TYALGUM, NSW

Inside, a representative of the video generation hones his gamesmanship while two old-timers take a breather from their daily practice of other, more venerable skills: Conversation, Reminiscence, Chinwaggery and, of course, Gossip. Pretty much fixtures under the verandah of the Tyalgum Store, in the hills of northeast New South Wales, Jack (left) says "We're here every day and there's not much we don't find out about. Whatever we miss one day, we catch up with the next."

Appreciative of an audience other than Jack, Aub began to tell me all about himself just as the bloke next door started to mow his nature strip. Aub kept right on talking as the lawnmower roared around our feet. I think he was telling me what he used to do for a living, but I never heard a word of it and I was too polite to ask him to repeat it, so now I don't know.

JACK KRELLE AND FRIENDS • RAINBOW, VICTORIA

Just about every country town has one. In Tyalgum it's in front of the general store;
in the Victorian Mallee town of Rainbow, it's outside the butcher shop. Retired farmer
Jack Krelle (right), eightysomething, calls it "The Seat of Knowledge," and likes to sit there
having what he calls "informal council meetings" with his friend Brian Solly and whoever else
happens along. They all reckon that more sense is talked there than in the council chambers
anyway, and they're probably right.

LESLEY STYLES, WITTENOOM PICTURE GARDENS • WITTENOOM, WA

In 1955, Lesley Styles and two female companions took a 42,000 km working holiday around Australia in a 1938 Chevy ute named Laura. She earned her share of the expenses through painting and signwriting, and later wrote and published a colourful account of the journey.

She now divides her time between Kalbarri, on the mid-west coast of WA, and Wittenoom, in the Pilbara. She used to run a gallery there, but now paints mainly on commission.

Many years ago, at the request of the owner, "a volatile Hungarian" named George Toth, she decorated the now-abandoned Wittenoom Picture Gardens with painted palm trees.

The old picture gardens were the scene of many fond memories in the boom days of Wittenoom. "There was the time," she recalls, "that *The Ipcress File* got rained out three nights in a row. The first night the audience saw the beginning of the film, the next night they saw another 20 minutes or so, and the third night they saw a bit more, but then the rain just came down so hard you couldn't even see the screen.

"Well, everyone sat there until they were absolutely soaked, but George vowed that he had to send the film back the next day or the distributor would start sending him second-rate stuff. So we never did see the end of the movie, but some bright spark went to the town library and found the book, and everybody in Wittenoom passed it around and read the ending for themselves."

HELENE SOTER AND DAUGHTER, KITRI • WITTENOOM GORGE, WA

Helene Soter was born and grew up in the former asbestos-mining town of Wittenoom. At 17, she met a farmer from New South Wales, and married him at 18. They travelled around the world and settled on a property in NSW before eventually parting ways after about ten years.

In 1983 she came back to Western Australia and at the age of 27 found herself driving 85-tonne ore trucks at a remote gold mine on the edge of the Great Sandy Desert. While there she met her current partner, and in 1986 they returned to Wittenoom and took over the general store and service station.

Since the closure of the asbestos operations in 1966, Wittenoom's population has shrunk from around 2000 to less than 100. Despite passionate resistance from its remaining residents and the fact that the town is a major tourist gateway to the remote, spectacular gorges of the Hamersley Ranges, the WA government has waged a protracted campaign to close it down because of possible health risks from leftover mine waste. Both to preserve her livelihood and maintain her connection with the land she loves more than any other, Helene has played a leading role in the battle to keep Wittenoom alive.

"I allus has wan at eleven"

Traditional Carlton and United Breweries advertising slogan

Bill Ketteringham has been the Cue garbage collector and power station operator for just over 20 years. "I came up here and the shire clerk told me he could only give me a fortnight's work, so I said 'Well, that's better than nuthin.' Then the two fellas who had the job full-time got killed in a motorcar accident, so I got the job permanent, and I'm still here."

Every morning when he knocks off from his garbage round, about ten o'clock, he stops by the local general store for morning tea – a single large bottle of Emu Export Lager, drunk from a white china cup.

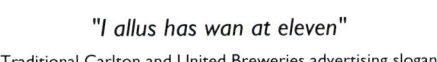

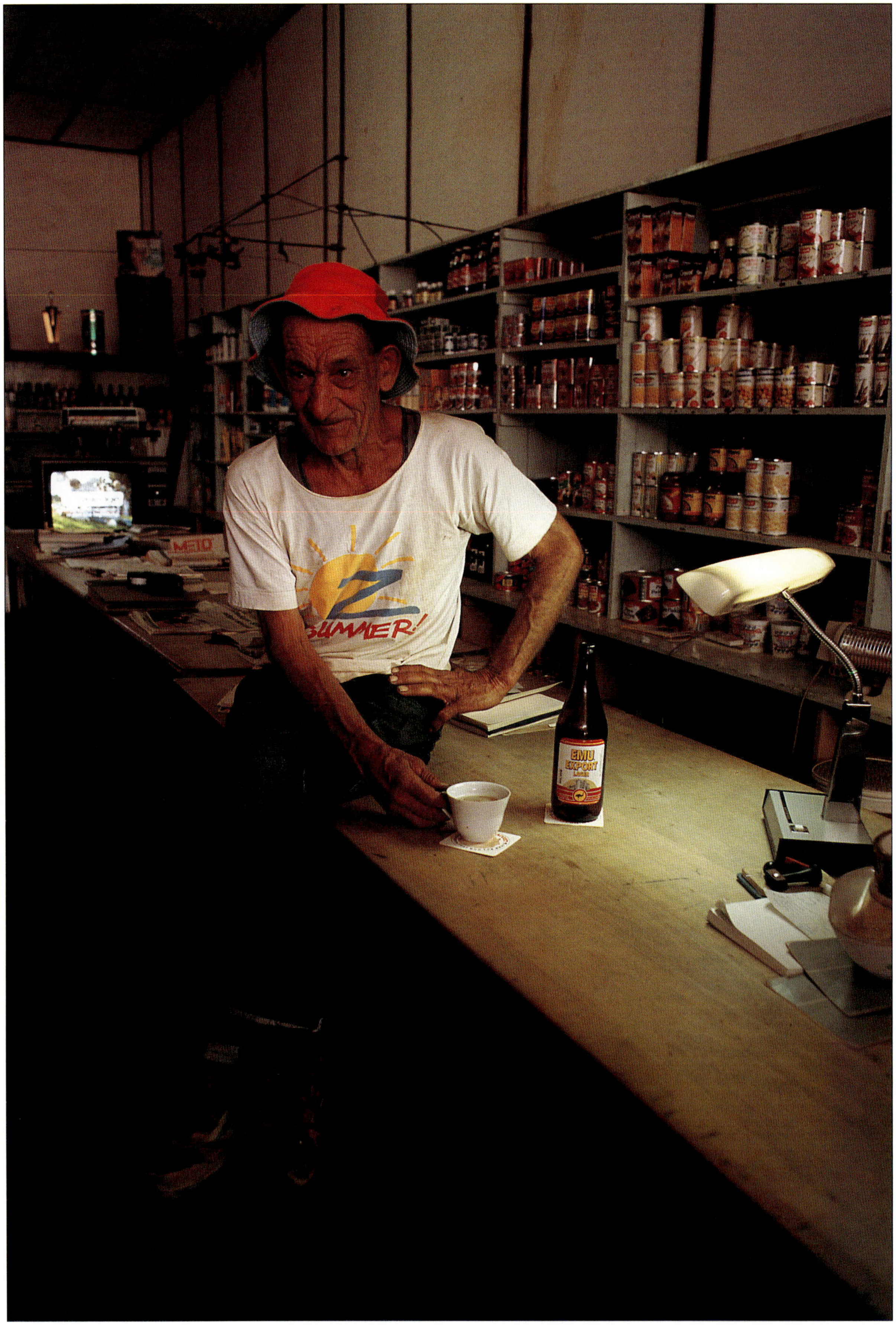

BILL KETTERINGHAM • CUE, EAST MURCHISON, WA

GRAEME "D-D-D-DAVO" DAVIDSON AND HIS PET GALAH, "PIGDOG" • GREGORY HOTEL, NORTHWEST QLD

One of Queensland's most remote pubs features cold beer, expensive fuel, a sublimely beautiful river
beside which to camp, and a cheerfully stuttering publican with a t-t-toothpicking cockatoo.

BRETT, DAVID AND RICHARD POLLOCK
WOOLEEN STATION, WA

A few years ago (and against his better judgment,
given the state of the wool and wheat markets),
Brett Pollock bought into "a magic bit of dirt" –
an historic Murchison district station with
200,000 hectares, 12,000 sheep, and a huge dry
basin that turned into a lake during good seasons.
What he got for his money was hard work, high
anxiety, and the best life he's ever known.

He is pictured here with his sons, inside an old
wooden hut in a distant corner of the property.
It was early summer, and the sun was making the
iron roof snap and crackle. When I wondered
aloud about the temperature outside, Brett
laughed: "What do you want to know that for?
When you find out, you'll only feel hot."

BILL PIGDON, BELL'S EMPORIUM • CUE, WA

For many years, Bill Pigdon was the storekeeper at Big Bell, a famous Murchison district gold mining town. When the mine there closed in 1955, he moved to Cue to manage Bell's Emporium, an old-fashioned general store established before the turn of the century. He later purchased the store.

Today, apart from a few splashes of modern advertising, the premises are pretty much as they've always been, with basic drygoods and foodstuffs arranged neatly on hardwood shelves running the length of the shop. In its heyday, Bill recalls, they also sold "men's wear, women's wear, pharmacy and fancy goods."

I first spotted Bill outside the store at 7:30 one morning, sweeping an already-spotless footpath. He told me he was 78 years old, and about to celebrate his 50th wedding anniversary. A couple of months later, he sent me a note in handwriting that looked like spider footprints and that said, in part: "Our anniversary must have been pretty good, judging by the Sunday morning condition of some of my mates and myself."

1991 AFL GRAND FINAL TELECAST • GASCOYNE JUNCTION HOTEL, WA

The Junction Hotel is a two-room, two-bowser pub set amid green grass and flowering bougainvillea in a wide spot in the road 175 km east of Carnarvon. On the 28th of September 1991, everyone in the district converged on this little oasis to watch the West Coast Eagles make history in their first-ever Australian Rules Football grand final, played against perennial champions Hawthorn.

   Alas, it was history poorly written, and in Gascoyne Junction the only giddiness was to come from fermented hops, as the grim-faced locals drank themselves deeper into misery with every Hawthorn goal, of which there were many. At three-quarter time, the publican, Bill Stocks (right), was so depressed that he went to bed, pulled the covers over his head, and could not be roused for the rest of the day. No doubt the afternoon unfolded differently the following year, when the Eagles actually took the flag.

ABORIGINAL FOOTBALL CARNIVAL • LAJAMANU (ABOVE) AND LARAMBA, NT

Some compare sport – especially football – to religion. Indeed, it is an elemental part of the Australian way of life in the same way that ritual and tradition underpin the Aboriginal world. Today, football is a popular ceremonial activity for many Aborigines, who often travel great distances to engage in this modern-day form of tribal warfare. Even the youngest aspire to one day dress as warriors

GOAT RACE • COOLABAH, NSW

Goat racing is a malodorous form of organised mayhem that is gaining many followers on a country circuit worth more than $25,000 a year. In a meeting which we attended one Queen's Birthday Weekend on our way through central New South Wales, chariots driven mainly by children wearing bicycle helmets made a terrible mess of a dusty 50-metre track, ricocheting off or becoming entangled in the rails and each other before hurtling over the finish line and screeching to a halt just metres short of a large patch of thorny scrub. As a safety measure the organisers had thoughtfully set up a sturdy farm gate on the edge of the scrub. A few goats tried to scale it to the detriment of their jockeys, but none actually succeeded. There were races involving trained goats and wild goats - the latter supposedly more unpredictable and dangerous – but frankly it all looked equally lethal to those of us bemusedly munching barbecued goatburgers on the sidelines.

HARTS RANGE PICNIC RACES • HARTS RANGE, NT

CRAB RACE, SNAKE CREEK TURNOUT • NEAR NORMANTON, QLD GULF SAVANNAH

Every July the residents of Normanton and Karumba gather halfway between the two towns, on a patch of scrub that used to be a bush racetrack back in the '40s and '50s, for a weekend "turnout" that features not only a token horse race, but also touch football, crab tying, tugs of war, iron man contests, and various competitions that involve drinking beer and taking one's clothes off. The longest event is the crab race. The quickest and most unpredictable are the little dog and big dog races. The most unusual is "Chook-Poo Bingo," wherein punters purchase $5 squares on a large bingo card lying on the ground inside a wire coop. Once all the squares have been sold, a chicken is placed in the coop and left to wander around. Whoever owns the first square pooped on gets the jackpot. For variety, some years they use a horse in a paddock.

At Harts Range, about three hours northwest of Alice Springs, they start with a basic bush horse race over a long weekend and add various games of skill to make up a "Family Sports Day" halfway through. Lizard races, high jumping and three-legged races all figure in the programme, but the blue ribbon event for all comers is the Harts Range Mile, a footrace which is sometimes contested in novel ways (TOP LEFT). Among the ladies, the Bull Tail Toss (TOP RIGHT) carries the most prestige.

STATION GATE NEAR MATARANKA, NT

STATION GATE NEAR KATHERINE, NT

FRIENDLY WARNING I • WYNDHAM, EAST KIMBERLEY, WA

FRIENDLY WARNING II • MARBLE BAR, EAST PILBARA, WA

THE HAPPY HIGHWAY • NEAR IRON KNOB, SA

COUNTRY MAILBOX NEAR CARRIETON • SOUTH FLINDERS RANGES, SA

The Art of Incongruity.
Putting things where they don't belong –
buildings, roads, railways, exotic plants,
canals, fences, rabbits, cane toads,
even entire sheep stations –
is something that Australians
have always excelled at.

Of course there's a fine line between
the wrong reason and no reason at all.
Fortunately, one's more fun than the other.

SMILE POST ALONG MARBLE BAR-NULLAGINE RD • EAST PILBARA, WA

HEAD FULL OF ROCKS • NORTHERN TERRITORY

BIKINI CONTEST QUARTER-FINALIST
NEAR GORDONVALE, FAR NORTH QLD

MISS CLONCURRY SHOWGIRL 1958
CLONCURRY, NORTHWEST QLD

"*Nature made the Australian bush in one of her untidy moods,*" said Robin Boyd in a 1959 essay published in WALKABOUT.

It's a pithy description of the Australian landscape, much of which in its natural state has an incomplete look about it, as if the decorators had suddenly got sick of what they were doing and gone home. Curiously, the same theory seems to apply to much of our manmade scenery.

PHIL MARSHALL DRIVE NEAR CANIA DAM, SOUTHEAST QLD

SILVER CITY HIGHWAY NEAR TIBOOBURRA, NSW

PAINTED TREE • WYNDHAM, EAST KIMBERLEY, WA

Art imitates nature and vice versa in these contrasting views of dead trees.
One enlivens the backyard landscape of a house on Western Australia's northern frontier, while others inhabit a scene designed by a surrealist.

PAINTED BACKDROP • LAKE GREGORY, WA

DEPARTURE LOUNGE • MULAN AIRSTRIP, WEST TANAMI, WA

DEPARTURE LOUNGE • SHARK BAY AIRPORT, WA

MATING SEASON
CHILLINGHAM, NORTHEAST NSW

I think it is only fair and honest to admit that among the English-speaking nations with which Australia likes to compare herself she is very high on the list of conspicuous ugliness.

Around 1960, the noted architect, Robin Boyd, coined the term "Featurism" to describe the Australian passion for artificially – and often hilariously – enhancing what started out as a perfectly splendid natural environment.

"Featurism," he says, "is by no means confined to Australia or to the twentieth century, but it flourishes more than ever at this place and time. Perhaps the explanation is that man, sensing that the vastness of the landscape will mock any object that his handful of fellows can make here, avoids anything that might be considered a challenge to nature. The greater and fiercer the natural background, the prettier and pettier the artificial foreground."

THE AUSTRALIAN UGLINESS (1960)

BRICK VENEER CARAVAN • WYNDHAM, WA

Featurism comes in a variety of forms, some more elaborate than others.

KURT BRASCHE AND "BRUNO" • NORTHCLIFFE, WA

Amid the sylvan charms of Northcliffe, in the far southwest corner of Western Australia, expatriate Victorian and jack-of-all-trades Kurt Brasche has devoted the last few years to a rather special backyard beautification project. After Christmas in 1990, he found himself in possession of an excess of beer bottles, and decided to build a wall with them.

  Each panel takes about 15 bags of bottles. By the end of 1991 he had completed three panels, and was about to start on a fourth when the local council decided the fence was an eyesore and should be pulled down. But everyone in town objected, reckoning the wall had become a tourist attraction, so it stayed, and grows a little longer every time Kurt gets some more bottles and a few spare bags of cement.

GERRY'S GARDEN • WHYALLA, SA

Gerald Pickhaver died in 1987, but his artistry lives on in the front yard of No. 12
Barter St. in the drab industrial town of Whyalla, where over the years he assembled
a colourful cement menagerie. Even the teeth are real, gleaned from the local abattoir.

MURAL ON SUPERMARKET WALL • COOBER PEDY, SA

MURAL ON SUPERMARKET WALL • ALICE SPRINGS, NT

WINDOWS DOWN AND SHIRT OPEN

Windows down and shirt open, you career through the great red blur of land where no bird flies, no animal breaks its meagre cover, no event feeds the eye. The hot wind funnels in across your face, fills your mouth and tears your hair at its very roots. You breathe insects, dust and the taste of baked spinifex, and with your arm out the window, redder than the other by half, and a few minutes from a real good burn, you drive on and on with the peculiar lack of expectation that comes from knowing there is no town just around the bend. Indeed, there is no bend at all. Truly an open road, this might go on unbroken to sunset.

But if a car should pass – a pastel dust column so far off, a battered Toyota in the second it blasts by to choke you – you'll wave or raise one finger minutely from the wheel in salute. Not because you're polite or friendly now that you're out here in the bush, nor that you're even grateful to see another human face in this vast calm, but because that pink colour and passing truck is an event, and out here you just can't bring yourself to let an event go by unheralded.

The wind trills in your teeth. The road unrolls itself. You wouldn't be surprised to discover that it goes on like a dream forever. World without end, amen. Not comforted, perhaps, but certainly not surprised.   TIM WINTON

BULLCATCHER AND BULLDUST, EL QUESTRO STATION • EAST KIMBERLEY, WA

Though neither, perhaps, is unique to Australia, both the bullcatcher and bulldust are highly-evolved outback phenomena.

In an age of recycling, the bullcatcher represents a zenith of sorts. Used to catch scrub bulls over perilous terrain, it is the stockman's rally-car, and usually bears no resemblance to the cab and chassis it originally was, having been reinvented from scavenged parts at practically every stage of its battered life.

Bulldust is what you get when it hasn't rained for months, and an endless parade of trucks and 4WDs have pulverised the dirt and clay to the point where the road actually moves underneath you. Driving is like skiing in deep powder snow. The dust follows you like thick smoke, permeating everything. For all the good that rolling up the windows and closing the vents will do, you might as well be in a bullcatcher.

(LEFT) STATION TRACK, ROY HILL • EAST PILBARA, WA

Apart from a ring road around the continent, a strip of bitumen up the centre and a well-developed circulatory system of blacktop highways along parts of the coastal margin, Australia is mainly stitched together with threads of dirt, sand, mud, rock and gravel, most of which will never appear on any map. Basically, a road is wherever you find two wheel-tracks.

ROAD TRAIN, NGUMBAN CLIFF
GREAT NORTHERN HWY, WEST KIMBERLEY, WA

Scenery. In the endless outback, they often put
up a sign to tell you when it's coming, so you
don't miss it. For the long-distance driver, at
least a nice stretch of landscape is something to
look forward to at the end of an afternoon of
the same old roadside attractions: skid marks,
trashed vehicles, tyre carcasses curled up like
giant black pencil shavings, bulldozed bullocks all
blown up with death, and the glittering rem-
nants of broken windscreens.

(GATEFOLD, OVERLEAF)
TABLELANDS HIGHWAY
BARKLY TABLELAND, NT

*Nothing is more mournful than the great plains,
treeless and grassless, that are to be found all
over Australia.*

*The pallid sky without a cloud oppresses you
with its intolerable burthen, and your eyes ache
with looking towards the viewless horizon smoking
like a cauldron.*

Often there is no sign of life whatever.

Francis Adams, THE AUSTRALIANS: A SOCIAL SKETCH (1893)

ROAD TRAIN, DUNCAN ROAD
EAST OF HALLS CREEK, EAST KIMBERLEY, WA

Beef on the hoof becomes meals on wheels,
in six decks on the way to market.

The triple road train is one of the most
awesome and, for the traveller forced to
share the same road, fearsome sights in the
outback. Sixty spinning wheels throw up a
lot of dust and flying stones, and if it's coming
in your direction, the best way to deal with
such mayhem is to pull off the road and wait a
little while. As for overtaking one of these
behemoths . . . don't even think about it.

STATION TRACK, TANAMI DOWNS • TANAMI DESERT, NT

Like rusty ribbons of corrugated iron, the minor byways of Australia's outback recede through uncharted plains of
spinifex and dwarf mulga. When the road forks or meets another, there will seldom be a sign to show you the way.
If you don't already know, you can only drive on toward the vanishing point, and find out for yourself.

KENNEDY DEVELOPMENTAL ROAD • CHANNEL COUNTRY, WEST QLD

No lines, no lanes, no limits. Despite the freedom they promise, many of Australia's bush highways are just bitumen bridges across a waterless ocean. Stray too far from the straight and narrow, and you'll discover just how limited your choices really are. The black track is often the only option.

CARPENTARIA HIGHWAY WEST OF CAPE CRAWFORD, NT

CAMEL, WOMBAT, KANGAROO • EYRE HIGHWAY, NULLARBOR PLAIN, SA

On permanent watch near the eastern entrance to the Nullarbor Roadhouse, where the big trucks hiss and grind, these cutout creatures have watched many a heavy load and weary head go past. It's a long (about 2400 kilometres) and lonely drive from Port Augusta to Perth along the Eyre Highway, a thin black thread connecting Australia's entire western third with what every one of its 1.6 million residents seem to call "The Eastern States," as if they formed another country altogether.

VICTORIA HIGHWAY NEAR KUNUNURRA • EAST KIMBERLEY, WA

Taking a bearing off the headlights of a semitrailer bound for Darwin, Venus, Mars and Jupiter point the way west.
If you follow them all night long as far as Broome, then turn left and drive for another 2500 kilometres,
you'll get to Perth without ever having left the highway you started on.

WORLDS UNTO THEMESELVES

The landscape of the Australian interior, the unpeopled and unmarked expanse that still exists in reality as well as in national myth, is so mystifying and surreal for want of something to measure it against. Where there is no house, no cow, no child to make the landscape background and supply some scale, the viewer, climbing up onto the roof of his vehicle, struggling to get a handle on things, is mesmerised, overwhelmed and almost drowned by colour, texture, graphic pattern. If the Antarctic has its terrifying "whiteout," then the outback has "redout" aplenty. A small stone in the palm can be mistaken for a topographical overview, and an aerial photograph for a mineral sample. In the midst of its immeasurable spaces, the land causes the human eye and mind to flounder. So much of the continent is an exercise in abstraction. It is either the best or worst place in the world for the embattled psyche, as much of our best art and fiction shows. Photographs of this landscape quickly become, like their subjects, worlds and ideas unto themselves, and ones not readily disclosed. Beautiful and terrible.

TIM WINTON

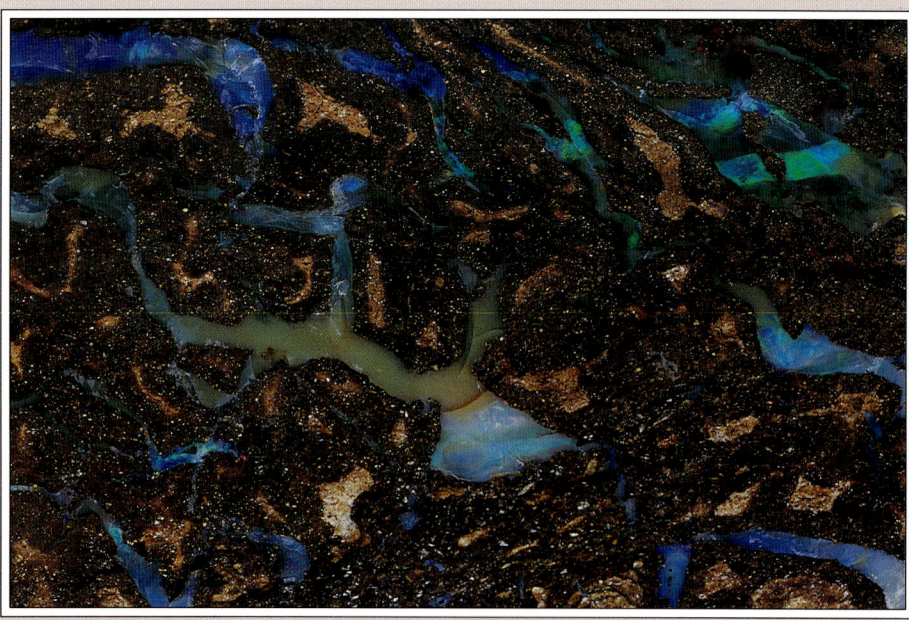

OPALISED ROCK • BOULDER, WA

A flooded Kimberley creek winds through mangrove scrub like the collapsed veins of a mineral sample
found in gemfields more than a thousand kilometres to the south.

DAMPIER CREEK AT HIGH TIDE • BROOME, WA

GRANITE BOULDERS ALONG COASTLINE • BICHENO, TASMANIA

In a *tour de force* of natural design, cryptic blooms of colour transform mere skin into exotic fabric.

(TOP) PAINT ON ABANDONED CAR BODY • BARKLY HWY, NT

(BOTTOM) KAURI PINE BARK • BLOOMFIELD, NORTH QLD

(TOP) LICHEN ON GRANITE BOULDER • EYRE PENINSULA, SA

(BOTTOM) UNAKITE • FINKE RIVER, NT

MUDFLATS NEAR PORT ROPER, NT

CRACKED PAINT ON ROADSIGN • HALLS CREEK, WA

CLAY PATTERNS ON TANAMI ROAD, WA

ERODED SANDSTONE • KENNEDY RANGES, WA

Under the open sky,
mud, metal, stone and wood
are seldom a match for
sun, water, wind and fire.
Eventually, all are etched
by the elements,
revealing hidden form and pattern.

TESSELLATED ROCK, TEA TREE BAY • NOOSA NAT PK, QLD

(RIGHT) FIRE-SCARRED BLOODWOOD • WINDJANA GORGE, WA

The delicate interplay of line, light and shadow brings to life the primeval architecture of three of Australia's oldest plant species.

PALM FROND • CARNARVON, WA

PANDANUS LEAVES • ROPER RIVER, NT

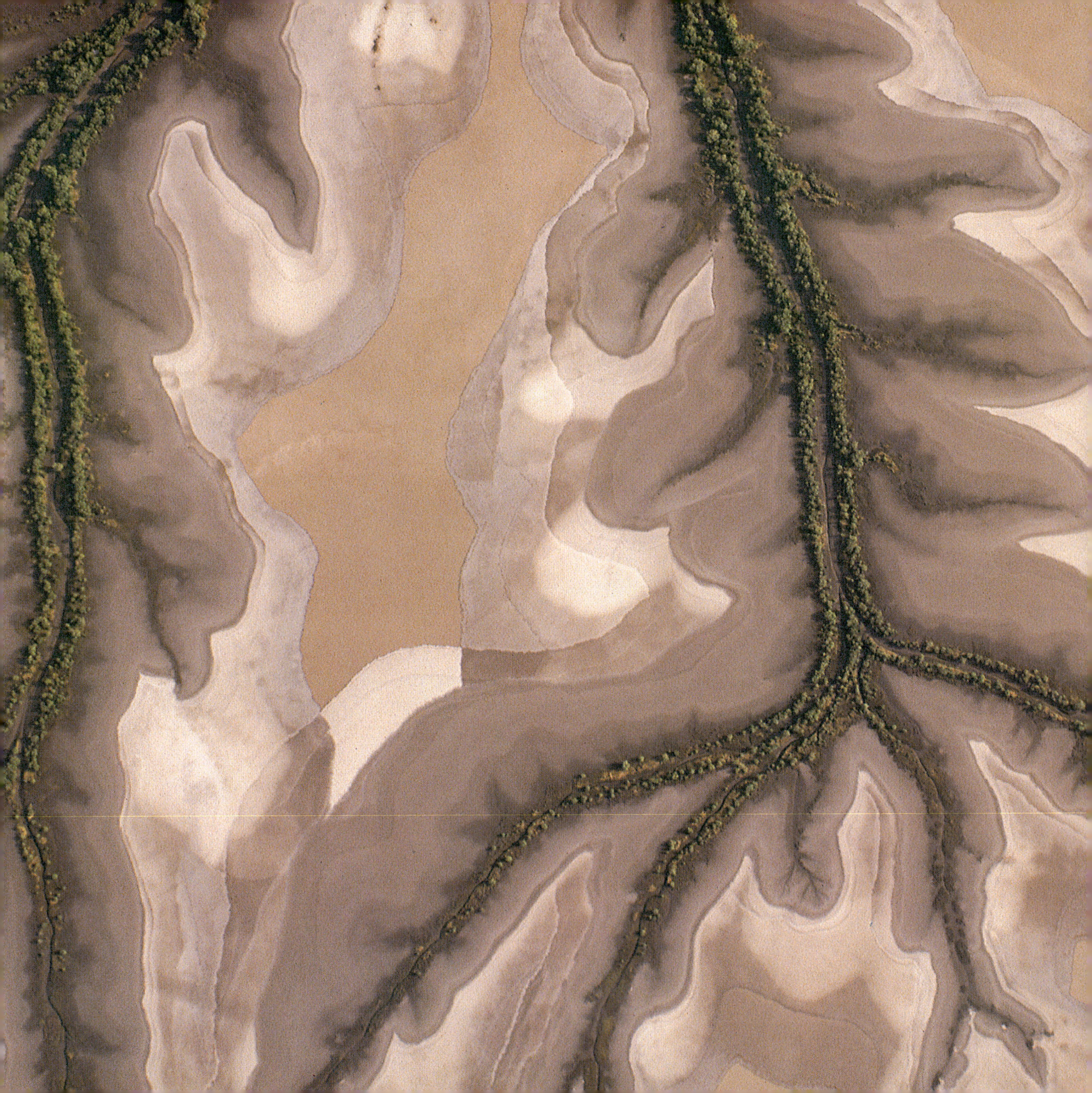

Crossing this ravelled shore
fern-patterns of the tides
frayed like my branching nerves

Judith Wright, from *Jet Flight Over Derby*
(COLLECTED POEMS, 1942-1970)

TIDAL MUDFLATS NEAR WYNDHAM
EAST KIMBERLEY, WA

Nature's fingers span vastly different distances on opposite sides of the continent.

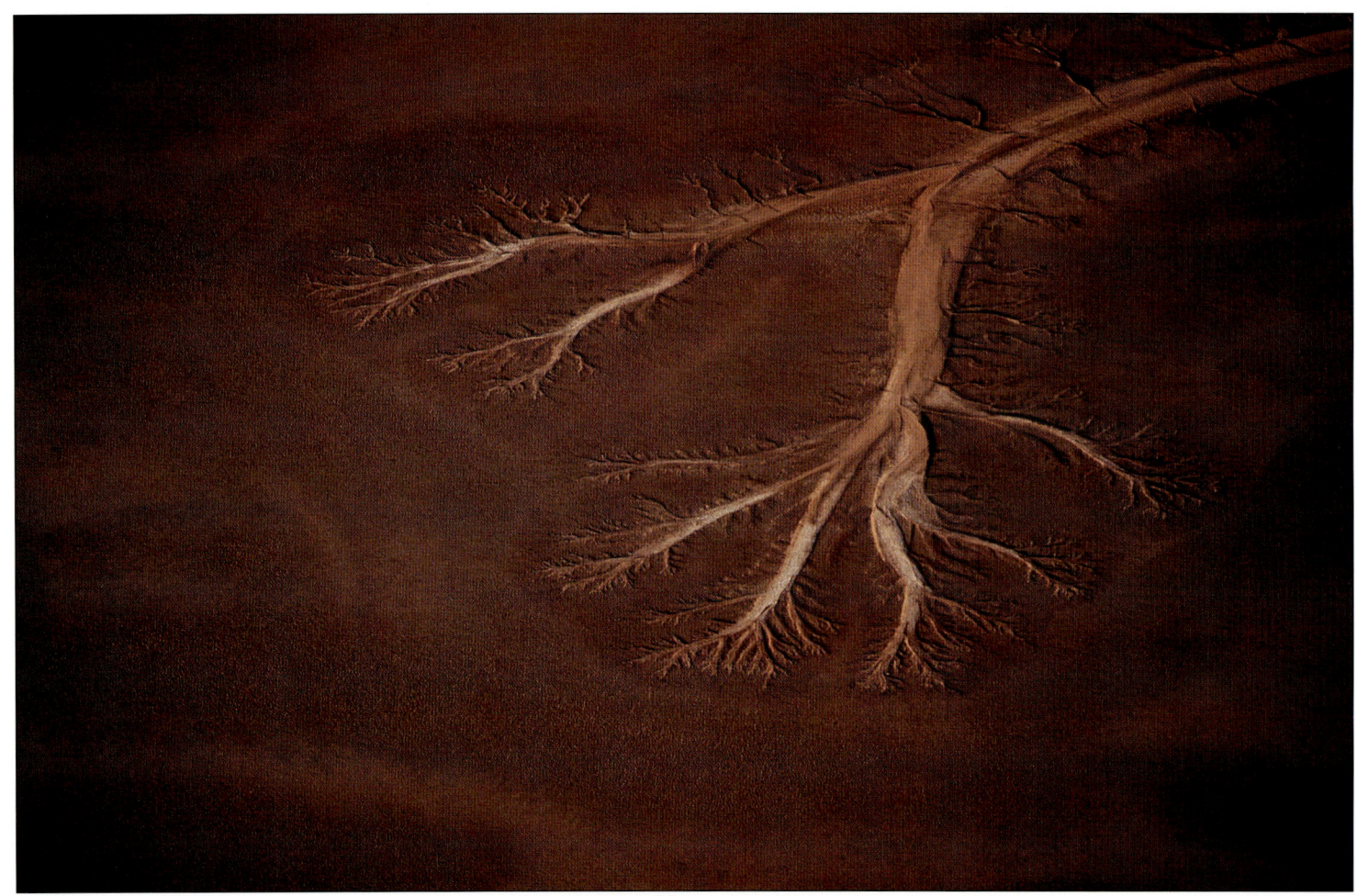

TIDAL MUDFLATS NEAR DERBY • WEST KIMBERLEY, WA

TREE ROOT AND SANDSTONE • CANIA GORGE, SOUTHEAST QLD

Animal, vegetable, mineral. Here, the feathers of a colorful native bird and the delicate fronds of a
primeval plant exhibit similar structure and pattern.

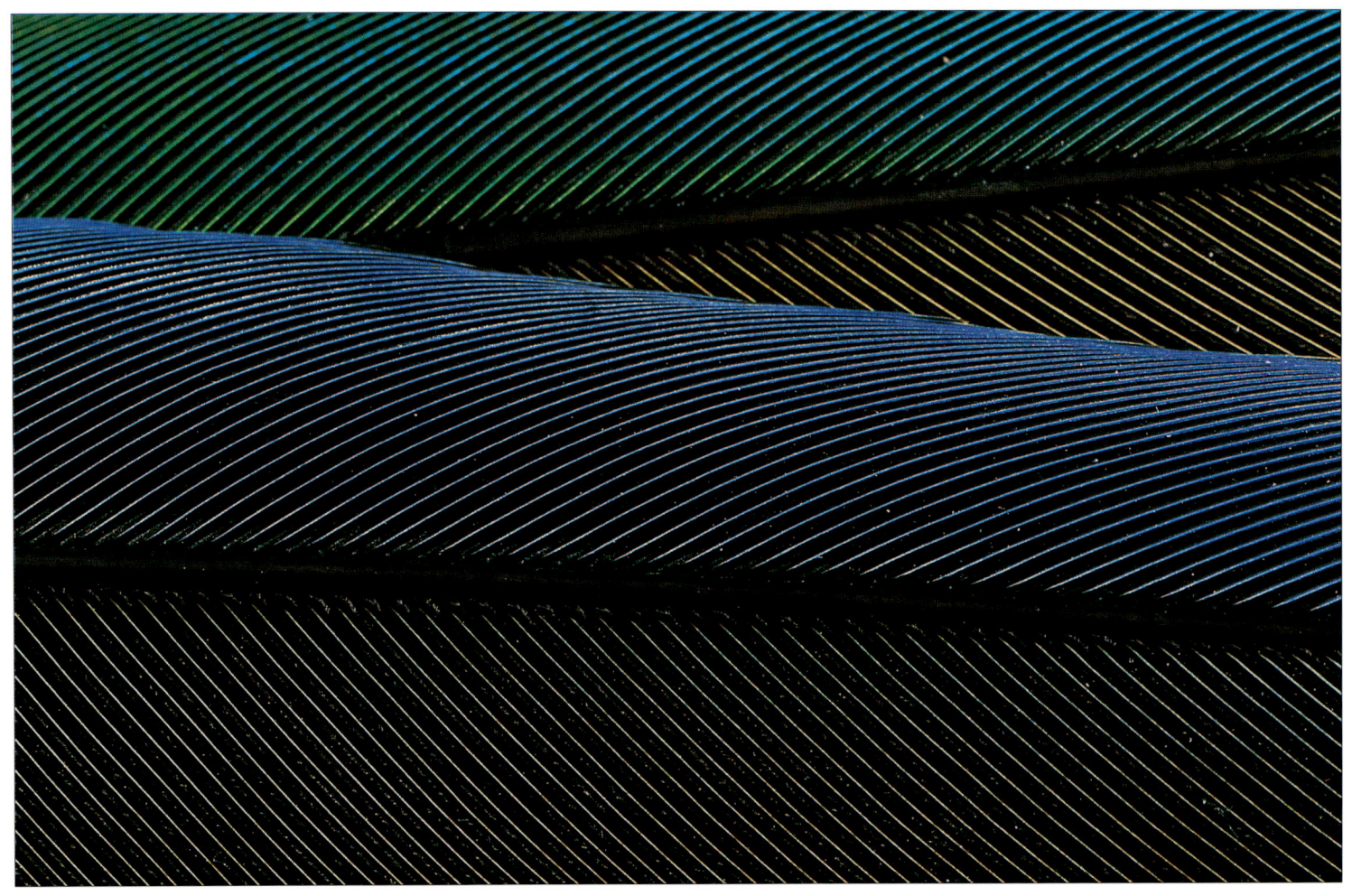

CRIMSON ROSELLA TAILFEATHERS • MERRIJIG, VICTORIA

TREE FERN FRONDS • CARNARVON GORGE, QLD

It's impossible to fully appreciate the Australian landscape without flying over it – although first impressions may be misleading.

In the four hours or so it takes to fly from southeastern Australia across to Perth or up to Darwin, what one mostly sees is an endless, sun-bleached canvas painted by an artist who selected almost all his colours from one end of the spectrum. There is umber and ochre and puce, off-white and khaki and olive drab. The patterns are random like camouflage, and the surface is so flat and unshadowed that every road, every roof, every river stands out distinctly. Up there at cruising altitude, it's hard to tell if you're looking at the real thing, or at a giant map of it.

It's not until you get down to a couple of thousand feet that things begin to change. Shapes distort, colours strengthen, contrasts grow more subtle, and identifiable content emerges from abstraction. All of a sudden, what looked like K-Mart art from 30,000 feet belongs on a gallery wall.

LOWER ORD RIVER NEAR WYNDHAM
EAST KIMBERLEY, WA

ORD RIVER NEAR KUNUNURRA • EAST KIMBERLEY, WA

COASTAL SANDSTONE NEAR BERMAGUI • SOUTH COAST, NSW

LAYERED ROCK • HAMERSLEY GORGE, WA

CONGLOMERATE CROSS-SECTION • KENNEDY RANGES, WA

THESE ARE THE HANDS

These are the hands that I somehow knew I would never have, the work-enlarged mitts of grandmothers and uncles, hands made not born. Fingers wide as paintscrapers. The nails black with soil, smelling of woolgrease and diesel, fish and animal blood. Hands that have no sex and little in them of race or class or age. These are the hands I come from, the bark-knuckled hands, spotted by sun and silvery with old scars, slips of the knife, hiccups of the winch and flywheel and fire. I'm not ashamed of my penpusher's hands, but I'd never say no to a pair of those.   TIM WINTON

COLLEEN McLAUGHLIN, BURNSIDE STATION
NEAR SPRINGSURE, QLD CENTRAL HIGHLANDS

Colleen McLaughlin has lived her entire life on Burnside Station, a 4000-hectare property established by her grandfather in 1884. All she ever wanted to do was work with cattle. Because there were no brothers, she rode beside her father as soon as she was able and, except for a few years when she was away at school or working elsewhere, the two of them ran the property together until he died in 1972.

Colleen was 45 years old at the time, and had never married. Her father was the only real partner she'd ever had, and losing him took a lot of getting used to, but as she says, "The land is my life. Once I realised that, I was able to get on with things."

For the last 20 years she has skilfully managed Burnside more or less on her own, with a little bit of help from her sister Lorna, and a lot from her dog, a black and white collie-cross named Shadrach.

The two sisters also run Old Rainworth Fort, a National Trust-registered collection of historic buildings located on a corner of their property. They donate any profits from tourism to the old people's home in Springsure.

(LEFT) ADAM PARBURY, TANAMI DOWNS
WEST TANAMI DESERT, NT

Fingers stained the colour of cattleyard dirt, Adam Parbury pinches the last bit of life from a hand-rolled cigarette before squaring up to another raceful of shorthorn calves awaiting branding and castration.

Manager of a large Aboriginal-owned cattle station just inside the Western Australian border, some 650 km northwest of Alice Springs, Adam was, like most Territory residents, born elsewhere.

In his case, it was the south coast of New South Wales, but he went bush while still in his teens and, apart from a brief stint in an agricultural college in England, has spent the past 20 years on cattle stations in central and north-western Australia.

DOROTHEA SWIFT AND HER LISTS • WITTENOOM, WA

Dorothea, a seventy-ish woman of Prussian lineage who lives at the upper end of Wittenoom with 17 cats, keeps lots of lists. "One is my diary, one is my daily worklist, and one is my exercise list. I do over 1000 exercises every morning to keep my muscles in tone. I don't like flabby things, especially on me," she told me.

"I had my handwriting analysed once, you know. I told the analyst it was for a friend, of course. Do you know what he told me? He said 'I would advise you not to associate with this person. This handwriting belongs to a mentally-retarded juvenile delinquent with criminal tendencies'."

We visited with Dorothea for several hours one warm September morning. A sharp-witted self-confessed alcoholic, she offered us "some refreshments" the moment we arrived, referring to the cask of cheap red from which she was topping up her coffee cup.

It turned out that she hadn't always been a compulsive list-maker. Back in the '50s, her own vaguely aristocratic background had led her into a lengthy dalliance with an English gentleman some 20 years her senior, who finally told her that if she married him he would give her a round-the-world trip as a honeymoon. They set off driving from London in about 1960 and, as she recalled, "The bloody motorcar started leaking oil the moment we got across the Channel."

They broke down with a collapsed big end somewhere in Turkey and spent three months waiting for parts, marooned in mid-winter in a little village 6000 feet above sea level. Eventually they reached Calcutta, and then Australia, where they inexplicably ended up in Wittenoom and Dorothea fell "unintentionally pregnant," and had her first of two sons. The husband eventually succumbed to a heart attack and Dorothea brought up her two boys in Wittenoom, where she still lends a certain exotic air to proceedings.

"Wittenoom is not a place, you know – it's a way of life. Very few of the people who live here are what you would class as normal, and there's not much that surprises us. In fact, a lot of us are either eccentric or alcoholic – or both. But we get by quite nicely, and even seem to attract plenty more just like ourselves."

HELEN NORTON AND *BLOOD FROM STONE* • BROOME, WA

Born in Melbourne in 1961, Helen Norton left home at 16 and spent the better part of the next ten years knocking around the back blocks of South Australia and the Territory, living on stations and in isolated bush camps and doing everything from professional shooting to fencing, cooking and road building. In 1986 her travels took her to the Northwest, where she married and settled in Broome.

Hands that once worked with wire and blood now wield brushes and paint. With them, Helen creates prize-winning paintings and sculptures based on her own bush experiences and on her exploration of the much-edited history of conflict between Australia's white settlers, the Aborigines, and the land itself.

Despite a lack of formal training, Helen paints with great imagination, wit and and style, and her work is held in collections all over Australia. The paintings range from the sublime to the shocking. Many are darkly comical, even surreal, with ironic references to significant events and personalities.

In many ways she believes the romantic notion of the Outback Hero is a dubious myth. "We've built our image on some mixed and motley foundations," she notes. "We want to be a nation but we continue to stumble over our past and our shady heroes."

"Blood from Stone" (part of which is pictured here is based on the Durack story. In the early 1880s Patrick and Michael Durack drove more that 7000 head of cattle from southwest Queensland to the Ord River, in the northeast corner of WA. The wives and children followed later.

"My focus here," says Helen, "is on both the spirit of the women, and their naive innocence as they followed their men to the harsh and lonely Kimberley wilderness, bringing with them implements of fine life and rural domestication that were quite irrelevant in this world."

PAINTING © HELEN NORTON 1991

STORIES UNTOLD IN A LANDSCAPE OF JUNK

To all Australia's pristine beauty we have brought the cargo cult, the landscape of junk. Stripped cars, tyres in trees like Christmas decorations, aircraft and farm machinery crashed and bogged and hilariously alone. The dead kangaroo propped up against the fencepost with the beer bottle in his paw. The farm mailbox – junk species *par excellence* – is a jaunty form of bush art, like the kero tin shack, the beer can regatta, the caravan homestead, the beerbottle wall. Out in all that landscape, it reminds us we're there. It's a form of whistling in the dark, a nervous reassurance. We are Hansel and Gretel leaving a trail. Each carbody is a story untold: a prang, a stranding, a change of mind, a family tiff, a buggered set of rings, a long walk in the sun. It's our spoor, this junk. This is most of what we work for and spend our money on, this stuff we leave by the roadside, hoping to be noticed, to be found, remembered at all. TIM WINTON

LOST DOG NOTICE • WILLS DEVELOPMENTAL RD, NORTHWEST QLD

In the middle of nowhere, the wrinkled, weathered panels of an abandoned car body announce the loss of a prized carnival dog.

(LEFT) TRUCK DOOR DETAIL • BARKLY HIGHWAY, NT

For over 50 years the Gill Brothers brought rodeo entertainment to rural communities all around Australia. In an unmarked turnout near the NT/Queensland border rests the sun-bleached carcass of one of their trucks, slowly shedding identity like a gum tree losing bark.

ABANDONED VEHICLE • ROEBUCK BAY, WA

A vintage motorcar rusts in peace beside tranquil waters near Broome.

(LEFT) WRECK OF THE *MAHENO* • FRASER ISLAND, QLD

Not many of the rusting relics littering the Australian landscape have a history as well documented as that of the 5400-tonne triple-screw steamer *Maheno*. Launched in Scotland in 1905, it was used as a hospital ship in World War I and as a trans-Tasman liner until the mid-1930s, when it was sold to the Japanese for scrap. While being towed to Japan in 1935, it was caught in a cyclone and washed ashore about halfway up the east coast of Fraser Island. Today it's a popular – if slightly perilous – fishing platform.

To go into rural Australia is to go into the past. There are any number of still-inhabited places where time appears to have stopped several decades ago, and the bush is strewn with abandoned houses, shops, farms and machinery. Yet surrounding much of this dereliction is an aura that is strangely alive, as if whoever was once there had just stood up and walked out one day, leaving the windows open and a half-swallowed cup of tea on the table.

MERILDIN RAILWAY SIDING, NEAR MINTARO
MID-NORTH REGION, SA

At a disused siding on the Broken Hill line some 130 km north of Adelaide, weeds encircle a hand-operated crane used for lifting heavy goods on and off railway trucks. Such sidings are located all throughout the grain-growing hinterlands of Australia. Because trucks are now the most common form of transport, however, many sidings are abandoned, and others mere mileposts on lightly-used lines.

ST VIDGEON HOMESTEAD RUINS
ROPER RIVER, NT

Located in the remote savannah of the lower Roper River, 6800 sq km St Vidgeon Station has had a succession of owners since it was first settled in the late 1800s. A harsh climate and extreme isolation, along with hostile Aborigines and an abundance of crocodiles, made life difficult for the early cattlemen; lack of finance hampered those who came later.

This homestead was the most recent of three attempts to establish a viable settlement on the property. Located near the river, it was built for the then-owner Jack Pender in 1964 out of concrete blocks made on site by former croc hunter and later proprietor of the Roper Bar Store, Dieter Januschka. The property was sold twice more in the next ten years, and abandoned for good in the mid-1970s. Though still owned by private Territory interests, it hasn't been run for pastoral purposes for nearly 20 years.

MURAL ON SUPERMARKET WALL • KATHERINE, NT   DESIGN © COLIN HOLT 1990

ABANDONED CAR • WANGARATTA, VIC

DRIVEWAY MARKER ALONG THE TANAMI ROAD, WA

Recycling has long been a boom industry in the outback. A discarded fridge makes a beaut mailbox on the road to Marree (Does the rock on top mean there's something inside for the postie to pick up? If so, would a cold beer be too much for him to hope for?) and an old Lawn Patrol marks the track to a mineral exploration camp in the Killi Killi Hills, about 50 km west of the NT border. " You can't miss the turnoff – just look for the white lawnmower," they told us.

STATION MAILBOX NEAR LYNDHURST, SA

Tidiness has never been a noteworthy feature of the bush. In fact much of the early history of Australia's backcountry was written in litter. Among the first signs of civilization along the overlander's track from Sydney to Melbourne in the 1840s was, according to one historian, a trail of broken bottles. Today, this wayside legacy consists mainly of things with wheels and wings.

ABANDONED UTE • BARKLY TABLELANDS, NT

ABANDONED AIRPLANE • BONNEY DOWNS STATION, WA

An air of unreasonable optimism surrounds some of the things that man has left behind.

CAMOUFLAGED COW • LIMPINWOOD VALLEY, NSW

In the hills of northeast NSW, a prospective buyer inspects
one of the leftovers from a country auction.

GHAN LOCOMOTIVE • MARREE, SA

In its heyday, the outback town of Marree was an important staging point on the
old Ghan railway from Adelaide; passengers changed trains there for Oodnadatta
and Alice Springs. Today, it's the end of the line.

VINTAGE TRUCK, MIDDLEBACK STATION • EYRE PENINSULA, SA

Interlaced fingers of western myall barricade an old Bedford truck on a sheep station near Whyalla.
The truck is a youngster compared to the yards themselves, which were constructed around the turn of the century
out of a picturesque local species *(Acacia papyrocarpa)* which can easily live to an age of several hundred years.

LANDOR

Mention bush races in Australia and most people will think of Birdsville, a tiny town in the desolate south-west corner of Queensland, where up to 5000 people congregate every September for a few days of drinking punctuated by the occasional horse race. The Landor Picnic Races are sort of the Western Australian equivalent, except they're neither as big nor as heavily hyped as the Birdsville Races.

One of the beauties of Landor is that it has never been connected to a town or a pub. The site itself is an isolated piece of country about 1000 km north of Perth and some 300 km inland from Carnarvon. The middle of nowhere, basically. It lies alongside Aurilla Creek, on the boundary of Landor and Mt James Stations, and is leased on a peppercorn rental by the Eastern Gascoyne Race and Gymkhana Club.

For 51 weeks of the year it is an abandoned assemblage of yards, sheds and shelters belonging to a variety of stations, clubs and individuals from all over the state, but every October all the absentee landlords show up at once and the ghost town comes alive for about five days, into which are squeezed a gymkhana, some polocrosse, a couple of race meetings, a dance, and a formal ball. For many of the local station families and their friends it is the biggest get-together of the year.

> *There's hardly a town to be called a town which has not its racecourse, and there are many racecourses where there are no towns.*
>
> Anthony Trollope, AUSTRALIA AND NEW ZEALAND (1873)

Racing at Landor is a tradition that started at the old station homestead in 1921 as an informal competition for stockmen and stock horses from neighbouring stations. The club

A comely racegoer eyes the form in the mounting yard.

was registered the following year and to this day it administers the meeting as a strictly non-professional event: only amateur jockeys and Northwest-bred horses are allowed to race.

But as one respected gentleman, a veteran of more than 40 Landor meetings, has been quoted as saying, "You don't come here for the blasted horses. The horses are just an excuse. You come here to see people."

During race week, dust trails converge on Landor from every direction, but many people come by light plane as well. When ours landed around 11 a.m. on the Monday, there were 16 other aircraft on the ground, parked every which way in the scrub at the end of a red runway. Over by the creek, about five minutes away, sprawled a chaotic encampment of trucks, horse floats, caravans, tents, bough sheds, bark huts, 4WDs, tin showers, chugging generators, and timber horse yards.

It was Day Four, and the atmosphere was exuberant but slightly hungover. Most of the camps were busy preparing lunch and getting ready for an afternoon at the track, which could be seen about a hundred metres away.

All around us people were scrubbing socks, boiling eggs, knotting ties, snoring, patching tyres, rolling swags, barbecuing meat, siphoning fuel, shaving, exercising horses, disciplining dogs, drinking beer, and putting on lipstick. There was even a bloke in full stockman's regalia riding a ten-speed racing bike around in the scrub.

The racing? Well, it got underway around a quarter to two, and even though it went on for about three hours, it seemed to speed past in a flurry of hooves and a cloud of dust. As it often goes with such events, there was an air of benign frivolity, fuelled ever so gently by a steadily-increasing level of intoxication on the part of almost everyone present. By 5:00 the crowd was as mellow as the sun, which had begun to sink into a reddish-brown haze on the other side of the track.

The racing? It was terrific, I guess. But like the man said, you don't come to Landor for the blasted horses. You come for the people. – BILL BACHMAN

Forward Ho noses in front as the horses near the winning post in Race Three. In years gone by, strings of station horses were walked to Landor – some as far as 320 km – where they raced, and then walked home again. The journey often took a week in either direction. Today they are trucked in from all over the district.

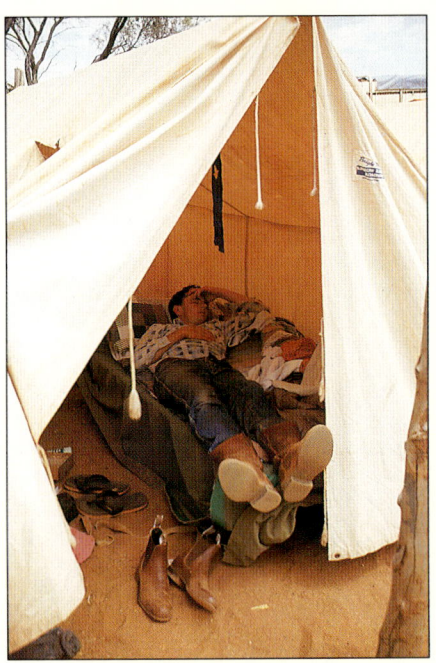

A pickled punter dreams of the next race.
For many, Landor is a continuous four-day
party, and beer is often consumed in heroic
proportions, resulting mainly in hangovers,
fatigue, and misguided betting.

"I've got the bloody flu, worse luck," claimed the fellow on the ground.
"I tried to get rid of it with a bottle of rum, but that didn't seem to work.
Maybe a nap will help sort it out." Except for a cut finger, there was nothing
wrong with his mate on the camp bed, but he tried the cure, too, just for the hell of it.

Perth youngsters Joshua and Luke Price
get cleaned up for the Cup Ball. In the old
days, humans and horses depended on
Aurilla Creek for water, but the creek was
often dry, and water had to be carted in.
Eventually a bore was sunk and hooked
up to an electric pump, and the campsite
now boasts open-roofed hot showers.

(LEFT) Home-made horse yards are just one of the features that give Landor a flavour all its own. Everything there has been financed and built by regular comers, and though tourists are welcome, they are neither needed nor particularly sought after as a source of revenue.

(ABOVE) Lunchtime in the Murchison District camp. Landor has always been a family affair, held during the spring school holidays, and Saturday's gymkhana is fiercely contested by the younger set. Many stations and groups from the Murchison and Gascoyne districts maintain permanent campsites – usually a bough shed that serves as a kitchen and dining area, surrounded by tents as required. Portable generators supply electricity to run the fridges, freezers and lighting.

On Cup Day, Race Five was a tight contest won by Rare Ebony. There is a full card of racing on each of two days. The riders are strictly amateur, many of them women. Though the racing is taken very seriously, the keynote at Landor has always been fun.

(LEFT) The Eastern Gascoyne Race Club Members' Stand is located next to the most important structure in the entire camp: the bar. In a good year, more than 600 people turn out for the four-day carnival, many from as far away as Perth and Broome. By the end of the last day, they will have filled the aluminium recycling bins many times over.

(BELOW) The only bookie in town did a desultory trade, which was no surprise considering he offered only WIN odds, and rather stingy ones at that.

(BELOW) Horses and jockeys leave the mounting yard before the start of Race Five.

(ABOVE) A young jockey waits for the next race in a shed festooned with streamers in anticipation of the night's Cup Ball, a red-dirt, black-tie affair where trophies are presented and the dancing goes on 'til dawn.

Carolyn Ryan of Geraldton places a bet on a Landor hamburger.

Inside the Members' Enclosure.

*The race card is still digital
in the old-fashioned way.*

RACE 2   Br.   KL.
1 Shillele   3 T. Hunter   76
2 Bold Impression 5 G. Brennan   73
3 Midnight Gift+4 B Mainwaring   73
4 Gold Letter   7 M. Nash   72
5 Reicky   1 T. Reick   73
6 Mr. Impressive   6 C. Furniss   70
7 Muggamurra   2 A. Green   71
        No 7   PLUS 1 KL.
        "5   "   1 KL

RACE 3   K1
1 Forward Ho   9 M. Nash   74
2 Rockador   3 J. Hollamby   74
3 Quindy

SKY, LIKE A SEA ABOVE

Outside the cities, overwhelming even the most astounding formations of land and distance, there is always sky, like a sea above.

The first thing the Australian notices abroad is the absence of sky; it accounts for our claustrophobia in Europe and Asia, our anxiety within our own cities.

A nation of coastal dwellers, yes, but so are those in the hinterland living beneath that other ocean. When you can see the curve of the earth, or imagine you do, out beyond perspective and scale, there is "sky all the way down to your boots," as someone once said, and you take a strange comfort in it, as if it's the only bearing you'll get on things in this life.

TIM WINTON

SUNSET OVER KING SOUND • DERBY, WA

(RIGHT) SPINIFEX PLAIN NEAR FIDDLERS LAKE • TANAMI DESERT, N

The land is here, sky high and blue and new as if you'd never taken a breath out of
and the air is new, new, strong, fresh as silver. And the country is terribly big and empty . .

D.H. Lawrence, in a letter to his mother (192

Europe has its peaks piercing the sky but we have the horizon.

Dame Mary Gilmore, quoted in THE STORY OF AUSTRALIAN ART
by William Moore (1934)

They may look like the Pyramids of Egypt to a termite, but the only peaks on the Tanami skyline are mere anthills when viewed from afar.

Ancient underground drainage systems known as fossil rivers have created nutrient-rich microenvironments in various parts of the Tanami Basin, which stretches northwest for almost 1000 km from Alice Springs. Larger, more mountainous anthills like these (built by termites with access to more fodder) and an increased concentration of small mammals often indicate the presence of such subterranean watercourses, which rely solely on uncertain skies for replenishment.

TERMITE MOUNDS NEAR FIDDLERS LAKE • TANAMI DESERT, NT

CHANNEL COUNTRY NEAR BOULIA • WESTERN QLD

Moistureless clouds mock parched landscapes in which a lone gum tree and an improbable roadsign look comically out of place.

Flat and dry for most of the year, the Barkly Tableland fans out to the east and north from Tennant Creek, covering more than 240,000 square kilometres and draining into the Gulf of Carpentaria. In a good summer wet season, runoff spreads quickly across its blacksoil plains to create one of Australia's richest grasslands.

The same monsoonal rains which nourish the Gulf Savannah can also flow southwesterly through an intricate, meandering network of normally-dry rivers toward the arid inland of Queensland and South Australia. A shallow basin three times the size of the Barkly Tableland, this "Channel Country" can become a vast floodplain in years of heavy rainfall.

BLACKSOIL PLAINS • BARKLY TABLELAND, NT

LAKE RUTH • TANAMI DOWNS, NT

Cattle normally graze where these clouds reflect in the waters of Lake Ruth, out on the western edge of the Tanami Desert.
The rainfall needed to fill the lake can be very unreliable, as this advertisement spotted many years ago in an Alice Springs newspaper attests:
"For Sale. One rain gauge. Two years old. Never used. As is, where is. Apply Mongrel Downs Station." (Tanami Downs used to be named Mongrel Downs.)

CHAMBERLAIN RIVER • EAST KIMBERLEY, WA

A mirrored blue boulevard here, the Chamberlain can also be a busy, muddy one-way street during the northern wet season, when sullen skies often dump a metre of rain in a matter of weeks. Once the monsoonal rains stop, most of Australia's tropical rivers revert to a series of deep, still waterholes like this one, and may not flow again for almost a year.

AUSTRALIA'S IRON CURTAIN

Almost all the visual grandeur of Australia is natural. True, there is more land here than people, more landscape than culture, and Australia is more of a continent than a country, but humans have been here 40,000 years and more. They have burnt, scratched, painted; they have dug and measured and built, but so little of what is left to show for all this activity can match the landscape or even fit into it.

It's not just a problem of our works being overwhelmed by space and distance, for many human undertakings here have been on an epic scale, and perhaps this is part of the problem. Our greater efforts have left the continent such environmental and aesthetic legacies as the eutrophic green of the Darling river system, the boils and scars and open wounds of the mining industry, the eroded red drifts of the ruined "cattle country," the terracotta bloom of the suburban outflow.

Where human Australia has been most successful is in the small and accidental, and even in the second rate. One of the greatest visual treasures we have is corrugated iron. All over Australia, especially in areas where timber and money were scarce, a cheap stopgap architecture arose that became beautiful and emblematic. Strong, light, and adaptable, corrugated iron gave us fences, dog kennels, roofs, whole humpies, cottages, shearing sheds, schools, town halls, churches. Fast disappearing in our cities until its recent rehabilitation, it has remained one of rural Australia's visual glories.

Texture. That's what corrugated iron has that other lightweight cladding lacks. There is something soothing in the channels of an iron wall; to the touch, it will never be the same twice, thanks to oxidation. Its colour develops, varies, keeps you guessing when rust sets in. Just imagine the Sydney Opera House in corrugated iron. Now that would be worth boarding a plane for.

Iron's acoustic properties can be vouched for by millions. What other cladding flaps so mournfully and eloquently in a hot wind? Iron gave our sheds voices; they are noisy long after their owners have departed. And what other roof can render an alighting bird an act of God? What better sound could rain make than to sing on an iron roof?

Corrugated iron is wonderful trickery, evidence of our makeshift culture. Think of the beacon in a red sea that a silver roof becomes to the traveller at the end of an afternoon. You see that silver roof, you roll into town and find stolid shopfronts, ornate and substantial, a permanent place, a refuge of human culture, and then you turn the corner to find that the town is a facade, the bourgeois stone and brick masking mere corrugated iron, like the new civilisation stretched skin-deep from coast to coast.

And along the rusting wall will be some kid with a stick, walking along – brrrrr – listening to the music of it, believing it was made for him alone.

TIM WINTON

ABANDONED MORRIS AND RAILWAY SHEDS • FORSAYTH, QLD GULF SAVANNAH

A motorcar long since put out to pasture adds a few brushstrokes of its own to the corrugated iron
and fibro-cement crosshatching on an old goldfields railway depot.

(BACKGROUND) BACKYARD SHED • BRONTE PARK, TASMANIA

(INSET) FENCE, WYNDHAM PICTURE GARDENS • EAST KIMBERLEY, WA

A rusty patchwork quilt. Swimmers in a rippling sea. The only time two pieces of corrugated iron are ever the same is when they are brand new.
The moment they actually become a part of something, they begin to change. The end result is always unique, the metamorphosis never complete.

MASONIC LODGE, CUE • MURCHISON GOLDFIELDS, WA

Dust to dust, rust to rust. Built circa 1899, this corrugated chateau was built entirely of galvanised iron and timber,
with a pressed tin interior. Ironically, perhaps, it is reverting to the colours of the earth from whence it came.

ST PATRICK'S CATHOLIC CHURCH • GEORGETOWN, NORTH QUEENSLAND

Decisions, decisions. Corrugated iron comes plain, painted or colour-bonded, with coarse or fine undulations, and flat or rounded ridges. In the bush, of course, basic is usually best, even if there's a higher purpose involved.

SHEARING SHED, WOOLEEN STATION • MURCHISON DISTRICT, WA

Looking more like an aeroplane hangar than a woolshed, this domed marvel, along with
the camp kitchen behind it at far right, are typical of many station buildings constructed
throughout the midwest of WA between 1917 and 1923 by the remarkable Alf Couch.
Carpenter, plumber and stonemason, Couch is best remembered for his innovative
construction techniques with corrugated iron. A number of his woolsheds, homesteads
and other large structures are still in use throughout the Murchison District. Most of his
curved roofs are entirely self-supporting, with neither internal timber frames nor pillars.
Some even feature glass skylights.

ABANDONED HUT • CAPTAINS FLAT, NSW

Patches scavenged from an old pressed-tin ceiling cover the eyes of
a miner's hut in the Monaro foothills of southeast New South Wales.

What could be described historically as Australia's throwaway attitude toward nature contrasts
dramatically with an almost instinctive ability to recycle and re-invent the domestic environment.
In the bush, things are rarely discarded – they're simply put aside for a while, often to reappear
much later, playing other roles. Old boilers come back as mailboxes; bed frames turn into station
gates and tin roofs into fences; sheds are even reincarnated as different versions of themselves.

INTERIOR OF OLD MINE OFFICE, DAY DAWN • MURCHISON DISTRICT, WA

At an abandoned goldfield near Cue, daytime constellations twinkle through the nail holes in a set of scrapheap shutters.

Corrugated iron was invented in England in 1829. Galvanising – dipping it in molten zinc to protect it from corrosion – followed in 1837. The first galvanised iron was imported to Australia in the 1840s, during the early gold rush days. It was initially used for rustproof mining utensils, buckets and so on, and in sheets was greatly prized as a cheap, strong and easily transportable building material.

  It quickly replaced bark shingles as a roofing material, and increasingly-scarce timber as cladding. In certain parts of the country, entire corrugated communities sprang up, like colonies of metal mushrooms. It wasn't long before the use of galvanised iron spread from the goldfields right throughout rural and suburban Australia. Over the years, it has been an integral part of many of our finest and most uniquely Australian architectural accomplishments, from the humble shed to veritable bush cathedrals.

FISHERMAN'S SHACK • CARNARVON, WA

One of corrugated iron's great qualities is its tendency to go awry. In any case, the concepts of vertical and horizontal aren't that important - the stuff works no matter how you use it.

LIBRARY • RAVENSHOE, NORTH QUEENSLAND

Thanks to handy supplies of base metals, many settlements in the Cairns hinterland were built predominantly of iron. This warehouse of wisdom is typical of the no-frills style of construction associated with corrugated iron.

HOUSE, SHED AND WATER TANK • HUGHENDEN, QLD

Although intrinsically monotonous, corrugated iron is one of Australia's most versatile building materials, and possesses many fine qualities. It's light and strong. It bends and folds, but doesn't warp, split, shrink or dry out. Ants don't eat it. It doesn't catch fire. It doesn't erode or crumble. It's waterproof. It can be nailed, screwed, wired, or soldered. You can dig it in, prop it up, or just lay it over the top.

Perhaps its only shortcoming is that it absorbs more heat than it reflects, which is really only a problem if you're inside. And ultimately, of course, it rusts – although that generally serves to improve its appearance.

1878
1916
CORFIELD & FITZMAURICE PTY LTD GENERAL MERCHANTS.

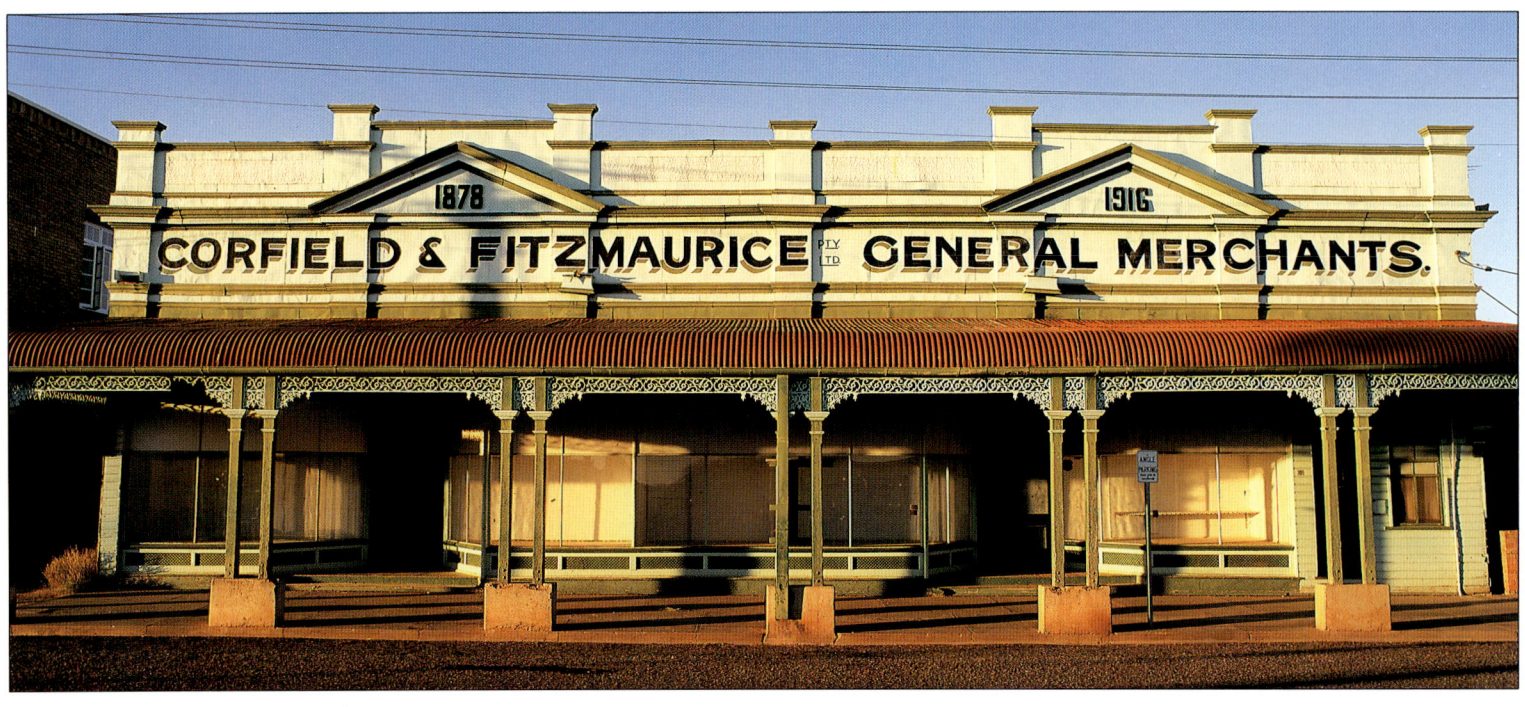

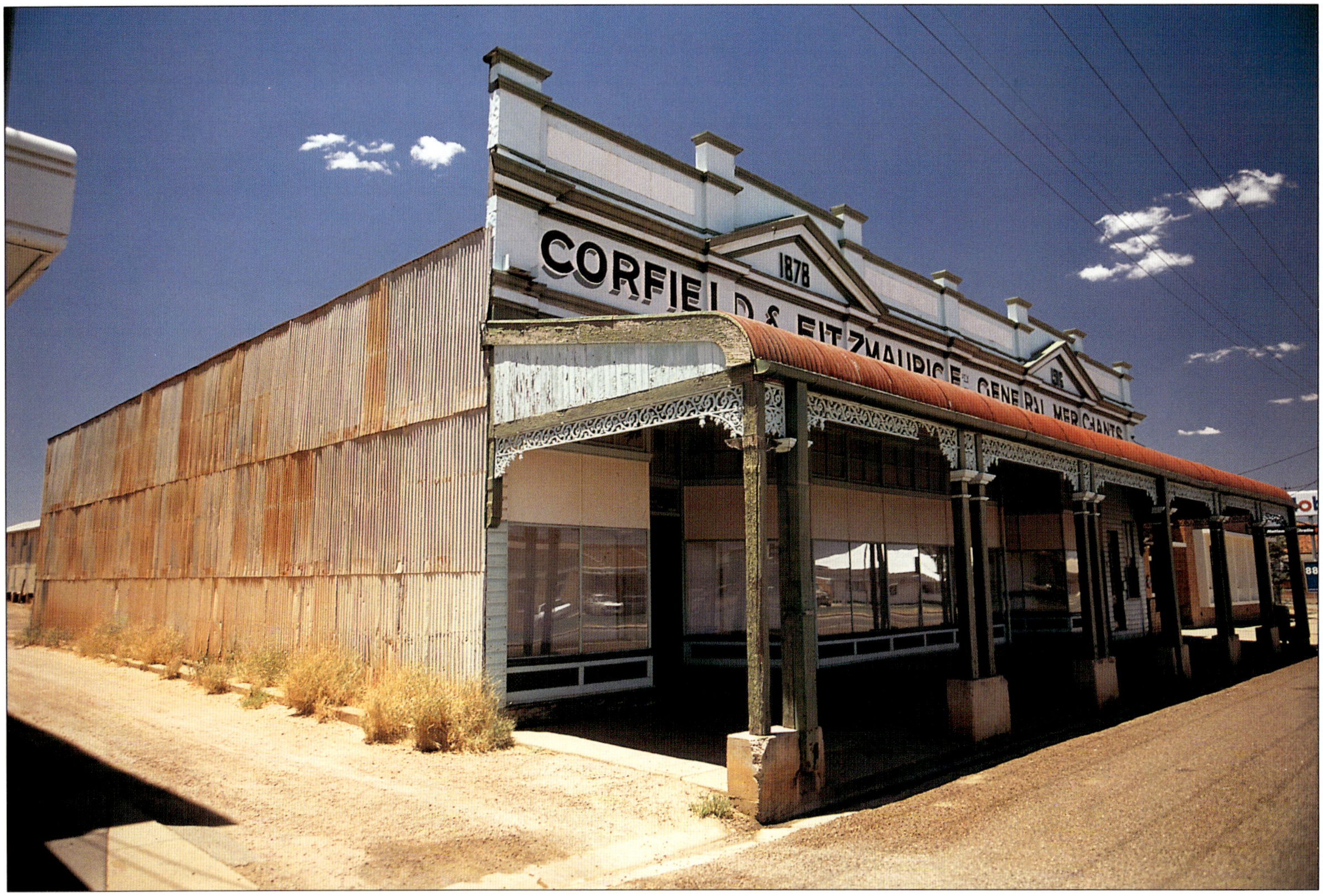
CORFIELD & FITZMAURICE GENERAL MERCHANTS
1878
1916

(LEFT) ABANDONED STORE • WINTON, QLD

Beauty is only skin-deep on this film-set store in central Queensland. Buildings with ornate facades and thrift-shop flanks and backsides are common throughout Australia, even today.

Corfield and Fitzmaurice were the third storekeepers in Winton. They first opened in 1878, and built the store pictured in 1916, after fire destroyed its predecessor. The store has been closed since 1989, but a group of local women is trying to raise enough money to re-open it as a tourist attraction. It still contains many of the original fittings, including a flying fox which carried money and sales slips between the serving counter and a cashier upstairs.

Corrugated iron can mimic the patterns and texture of the natural landscape - sometimes through colour of its own, sometimes through artful camouflage.

(TOP) PINDAN DUST ON HOUSE WALL • BROOME, WA

(MIDDLE) CORRUGATED IRON, VICTORIA

(BOTTOM) SAND DUNE NEAR PARACHILNA • FLINDERS RANGES, SA

FACES ARE LANDSCAPES OF THEIR OWN

Faces are landscapes of their own, I suppose. You can see the seasons in them, the passage of time, of conflagration and drought, of bounty gone, chances lost. You can see the nuggetty foundation coming through.

Genial, surprised, coy, proud, open, Australian faces all somehow manage to retain a terrible scepticism, the long stare within the expression which truly expects the worst. A matter of origins, I imagine. Many Aborigines show immense dignity, but there is a reserve there, an uncertainty borne of suffering. In the faces of stockmen, ringers, shearers, shopkeepers there is a cockiness, a swagger that belies a backlog of failure, defeat, and disappointment. There isn't the optimism you see in American faces, for there was no glorious frontier, no promised land, only a long, tough apprenticeship to the land that rendered people equally unequal.

Curiously, the land often renders itself in faces too, and it bears similar stories. Antiquity, attrition, fire, torrent, the grinding crash of continents. It is startling to see a body in stone, a figure in water and cloud. It is not only at night that trees become men and twigs the writhing bodies of reptiles. It makes the Aboriginal idea of Dreaming so much less quaint, your appreciation a tad less academic. The bush is a beautiful and fearful place. With greatness there is always some intimidation and some magic.

TIM WINTON

PAINTED GIRL • LAJAMANU, NT

Surely the world we live in is but the world that lives in us.
Daisy Bates, as quoted by Elizabeth Salter in DAISY BATES (1971)

(LEFT) PAINTED GIRL • THE CHANNON, NORTHEAST NSW

JIM AH QUEE • KARUMBA POINT, FAR NORTH QLD

Jim keeps a ramshackle kiosk overlooking the beach at the southwest corner of Cape York Peninsula.
When he sits at the counter, the waters of the Gulf of Carpentaria multiply in his blue eyes.

(RIGHT) JIMMY LENNIG • PORT ROPER, NT

Eyes like a spirit level of the soul, professional barramundi fisherman Jimmy Lennig stares out to sea
from a remote outpost at No 1 Landing, near the mouth of the Roper River. A Queenslander in his
early 50s, Jimmy started fishing here around 1980, after a life of knocking about.

  His camp consists of a big freezer, a few three-sided tin sheds, a couple of old caravans, a riverside
dunny with perilous underpinnings and a panoramic view, and a 44-gallon drum full of empty rum
bottles. It is home to him and a handful of other fishermen for about eight months of the year.

  Big barra and big bureaucracy have presented equal challenges throughout Jimmy's years on the river,
especially since the NT Government banned professional fishing from the lower reaches of the Roper,
forcing Jimmy and his men to set their nets outside the rivermouth, far from camp. If it weren't for the
isolation and independence of his bush lifestyle, he says he probably would have bailed out long ago.

DAVID ELLIOTT AND "ARNOLD" • QUAMBY, NORTHWEST QLD

Overshadowed by a hat as black as his dog, David Elliott was 11 when this picture was taken. The first time we saw him, he was barely visible behind the wheel of a two-ton flatbed truck parked beside the Quamby Hotel, a remote Gulf Region watering hole belonging to his father.

With Arnold riding shotgun on the passenger seat and a load of rubbish on the tray behind, he eased out of the driveway and started off down the road. He wasn't going all that fast, but there was a fresh breeze blowing, and before long most of the rubbish had taken wing, and was floating behind like the tattered tail of a kite. A little brindle pup gambolled in his wake, snapping at the falling confetti. There wasn't much left to dispose of by the time he got to the tip.

Considering the size of the truck, David was actually quite a good driver, and we later found out that he'd been at it since he was nine. As for lessons in tying down a load – well, they were still to come.

MRS A.E. ABBEY • FORSAYTH, NORTH QLD

"This house isn't what you think it is," she said, referring to the suggestive shingle over
the door. "Me son just thought it was a good name, that's all."

Forsayth is a small town at the end of an old mining railroad in the Gulf Savannah gemfields.
The underground water is so heavily mineralised that the houses "rust" from the spray
thrown out by lawn sprinklers, and end up looking like they're clad in long skirts that have
been dragged around in the mud.

TIM MACFARLANE, MOROAK STATION • ROPER RIVER, NT

It's not just the architecture of their faces, but a certain look in the eye that separates the people of the bush from their city counterparts. Often it is a strange mixture of pessimism and confidence – expecting the worst but at the same time knowing how to handle it and move on to the next thing.

For nearly forty years, Tim MacFarlane lived at Moroak Station, on the banks of a tropical river in the far north of the Territory. He was first taken there at the age of 18 months, and lived in a tent for two years while the homestead was being built from locally-cut timber. In 1985 he and his wife Judy bought the property from his parents, and for a while successfully ran a herd of about 4000 Brahman/Shorthorn-cross cattle over its 1600 square kilometres.

Compulsory de-stocking under the NT Government's controversial BTEC (brucellosis/tuberculosis eradication) programme, high running costs, and impossible interest rates put an end to all that in mid-1992, when the banks took the station. Valued at around $1.5 million, it sold for $400,000 to buyers who Tim describes as "a pair of multimillionaire American lawyers." All Tim has left now is a pile of debt and a small herd of Brahman stud cattle.

"It's happening all over northern Australia," says Tim. "All the little properties are being squeezed dry and sold off. Pretty soon the only landowners up here will be big corporations and blackfellas."

JUBILEE CHARGER • DELTA DOWNS STATION, QLD

When we met camp cook Jubilee Charger, he was working for a team of stockmen run by a fellow named Sandy Rainbow on an Aboriginal-owned cattle station in the savannah region of north Queensland, near the southeast corner of the Gulf of Carpentaria.

Open-air stock camps and dirt-floored bush kitchens are all the same to Australia's station cooks, who can put together a meal just about anywhere. A good sit-down lunch ("dinner," in bush parlance) consists of fresh corned beef served with black sauce (Worcestershire), red sauce (tomato), bread and butter, and boiled cabbage, cauliflower, peas, potatoes and pumpkin, with fruit and custard to follow and big mugs of black tea to wash it all down. Out fencing or on a muster, that might pare down to beef, bread and tea, so stockmen take their hot dinners whenever they can find them.

*Women punters abound on the racecourses, and the same faces
may be seen meeting after meeting. As a rule these punters
are middle-aged or elderly women . . . (and) there is no bashfulness
about these dames of the turf.*

Nat Gould, ON AND OFF THE TURF IN AUSTRALIA (1895)

PUNTER AT QUEEN'S BIRTHDAY PICNIC RACES • PARKES, NSW

Window of opportunity or barred cell?

These two men have differing outlooks on the rural way of life, one born of youthful optimism, the other of bitter experience.

At the age of 12, out hunting for mushrooms, Richard Pollock fell off his motorbike and broke his leg. It was several hours before anyone noticed he was missing, but it didn't take the crows long to find him. In pain and unable to move, he had to shout and wave his arms to keep them away until someone came.

Despite such traumas and the fact that wool and wheat offer no future for a young man these days, Richard reckons the best thing his father ever did was buy the historic pastoral lease where the family now lives. When he's away at school in Perth, all he thinks about is coming home to Wooleen. When school is behind him, all he wants is to be a grazier.

RICHARD POLLOCK, WOOLEEN STATION • MURCHISON DISTRICT, WA

The romance of life on the land isn't quite as strong for Ray Kennedy. Mind you, there's nothing wrong with where he lives and what he does. It's all the interference from Big Government and Big Business that's the problem.

Already turfed out of one cattle station – the jewel-like Millstream Station, over in the northwest Pilbara – by the State Government, Ray and his brother Murray live with their spry, eightyish mother on Roy Hill Station, a million-acre property north of Newman.

Sharp as filleting knives, the three of them have waged lifelong war with a variety of villains, bureaucratic and otherwise. Their latest vendetta is against huge mining interests which they maintain are seriously meddling with the Fortescue River, the floodplain of which runs right through Roy Hill. The Kennedys say that by interfering with the water table, the miners have reduced the carrying capacity of the property by some 50 per cent.

Despite the fact that it involves their very livelihood, to a certain extent they treat such skirmishing as fun and games – but occasionally their cynical good humour gives way to genuine vitriol.

"The bloody politicians and bureaucrats are ruining this country," says Ray. "I don't mind paying taxes, but we work hard for every penny we earn, and I don't enjoy seeing what we pay to the government being given away to all the bludgers who sit on their butts and expect to be paid for it. There's just too many bureaucrats wasting millions of dollars every day, and until that stops, Australia will never get anywhere."

RAY KENNEDY, ROY HILL STATION • EAST PILBARA, WA

JACK WESTERN, BOB MACKENZIE AND BRYAN STEELE • GASCOYNE JUNCTION, WA

Bush Mechanic is one of the most respected titles that can be conferred upon a man in outback Australia. It is practically tantamount to an academic degree or royal honours – in fact, few people are more important in the rural scheme of things. If you come to them with a problem they might need to order parts, but there's hardly anything they can't fix.

Along with his partner Bryan Steele and offsider Bob Mackenzie, Jack Western (at left) looks after the machinery owned by the local council and acts as general "fixit man" for the district. While the pace of life in Gascoyne Junction is not exactly hectic, that's the way Jack likes it: "I love it out here. There's always plenty to do, and better still, there's nobody to bother you while you're doing it."

(RIGHT) LANCE RAWSON AND LINDSAY LATTA • CHILLINGHAM, NSW

A beer and a smoke on the steps of the local general store is all in a day's work for these two battle-scarred fencing contractors in the northeast corner of New South Wales.

The man who takes wages does not at all feel himself
bound to lift his hat to the man who pays him,
or to acknowledge his inferiority by any outward sign.
But in lieu of such submissiveness there has grown
up a manly demeanour, combined with an open
smiling courtesy, which to me leaves very little
to be desired in manner.

from a letter written by Anthony Trollope in 1875

KEITH DELLAR
THE GRANITES GOLD MINE, TANAMI DESERT, NT

At one of Australia's most remote gold mines, some
550 kilometres northwest of Alice Springs, underground miners like Keith Dellar work seven-day,
four-week shifts before commuting back to home
bases as far afield as Adelaide and Perth for two
week breaks. On the job, they put in ten-and-a-half
hour days at depths of up to 300 metres, coming up
for a glimpse of daylight just once, for half an hour
at mid-shift.

   Australia's economy still relies heavily on traditional resource-based activities in the interior.
Including farming, industries based on soil or rocks
produce about 80 per cent of the country's exports.

DON KETTERINGHAM • WOOLEEN STATION, WA

*CECILY: I don't think you will require neckties.
Uncle Jack is sending you to Australia.*

Oscar Wilde, THE IMPORTANCE OF BEING EARNEST (1895)

Both in their mid-60s and similarly eroded by wind and sun, brothers Bill and Don Ketteringham also share parallel tastes in working class fashion.

Bill collects the garbage and runs the power plant in the old Murchison Goldfields town of Cue.

By his own account, Don has had "a hard life." A shearer, teamster, fitter's assistant and factory worker in his younger days, he walked off a wheatbelt farm during a drought in the early '50s. Not long after, he lost a lung, and then spent 33 years operating heavy earthmoving equipment.

The last 15 of those years were in the Murchison District where, says former shire boss Brett Pollock, he used to set off every day with half a dozen bottles of beer in the cabin of his grader. "Used to sip them warm, one after another, all day long," says Brett. "He was never drunk, but just couldn't do his job any other way."

When Don first went to Murchison Settlement, there were no houses, so he made a bough shed for himself. He reckons it was the only one in WA with a deepfreeze and a video recorder. When Brett Pollock bought nearby Wooleen Station, Don moved there as self-styled caretaker.

"I'm used to isolation," he told me in late 1991, just before he retired to Carnarvon. "Actually prefer it. On one job, I went 13 weeks without seein' anyone at all. So being out here suits me – I can live bush-style, and keep me own hours. I've got me chooks and pigs and birds (he kept 56 birds in his Wooleen aviary, including the lovebirds pictured here) to take care of, and I look after the power and water for the homestead, too. Every now and then I even get on the grader again."

BILL KETTERINGHAM • CUE, WA

WEST MACDONNELL RANGES NEAR GLEN HELEN, NT

According to Aboriginal mythology, much of the Australian landscape is populated
by huge hibernating beasts, and etched by the marks of their passing. In these pictures,
the tail of a giant reptile floats on the metallic surface of Lake Argyle, and the
backbone of a slumbering monster forms a mountain range out west of Alice Springs.

(LEFT) CARR BOYD RANGES, LAKE ARGYLE · EAST KIMBERLEY, WA

SNAPPY GUM NEAR HAMERSLEY GORGE • KARIJINI NAT PK, WA

In Australia alone is to be found the Grotesque, the Weird, the strange scribblings of nature learning how to write. Some see no beauty in our trees without shade, our flowers without perfume, our birds who cannot fly, and our beasts who have not yet learned to walk on all fours. But the dweller in the wilderness acknowledges the subtle charm of this fantastic land of monstrosities. He becomes familiar with the beauty of loneliness. Whispered to by the myriad tongues of the wilderness, he learns the language of the barren and the uncouth, and can read the hieroglyphs of the haggard gum trees (...) The phantasmagoria of that wild dream-land termed the Bush interprets itself, and the Poet of our desolation begins to comprehend why free Esau loved his rich heritage of desert sand better than the bountiful richness of Egypt.

Marcus Clarke, from his preface to the second edition of Adam Lindsay Gordon's SEA SPRAY AND DRIFT SMOKE (1876)

FIG ROOTS AND SANDSTONE, EDITH CREEK • KATHERINE GORGE NAT PK, NT

(LEFT) DRY DAM BETWEEN BOULIA AND WINTON
CHANNEL COUNTRY, WEST QLD

In contrast to Wolfe Creek Crater, and despite large-scale environmental sins elsewhere, many of Outback Man's efforts hardly make a dent in the earth's surface.

(BOTTOM LEFT) WOLFE CREEK CRATER
EAST KIMBERLEY, WA

A heavy-lidded eye staring from a sunburnt face, the second-largest meteorite crater in the world is 850 m across and 50 m deep, and lies about 90 km south of Halls Creek. The "pupil" at the centre is a large shallow depression where a stand of trees draws moisture through sinkholes in the gypsum surface.

   The crater itself is at least a million years old, and was well-known to the local Aborigines, who tell how one of the two serpents which created the winding beds of nearby Wolfe and Sturt Creeks emerged from the earth at the crater. It was officially "discovered" by a geologist on an aerial survey in 1947.

(RIGHT) ANGOPHORA BARK
CARNARVON GORGE, QLD

Sometimes nature mimics the human form with uncanny accuracy. Here, a perfect breast adorns the torso of a Smooth-barked Apple in the Central Highlands of Queensland.

NW KIMBERLEY COAST NEAR KOOLAN ISLAND, WA

These drowned mangrove inlets resembling giant natural marinas are part of the Buccaneer Archipelago. This remote coastline was first charted in 1821 by Phillip Parker King, and because of the treacherous nature of the waters, has been only scantly explored since and remains mostly deserted. King named the archipelago in honour of the English navigator and pirate, William Dampier, who landed briefly nearby in 1688.

Some parts of Australia are so isolated and undisturbed that their only history is pre-history. Despite our best efforts to imprint the entire continent, there are still landscapes where essentially nothing has changed since the first humans passed through them.

SANDSTONE BOULDER AND BLOODWOOD TREE
MANN RANGES, SA

Cracked like a prehistoric egg, this massive boulder bakes
under a cloudless sky in the foothills of the Mann Ranges, a
string of "desert mountains" in the northwest corner of South
Australia. Few Europeans are permitted to visit this country,
which is the traditional homeland of the Anangu Pitjantjatjara
people. These low, spiky ranges and the sandplains that
surround them are relatively pristine, and rich in sites of
spiritual significance to their Aboriginal owners.

A RURAL
RITE OF PASSAGE

In the city, belonging to "society" implies membership in the fashionable world of the privileged classes; in the country these days it usually just means adulthood.

Throughout rural Australia, thousands of teenagers still achieve that status via a time-honoured rite: the debutante ball.

In many of the closer-settled areas such rituals are a bit *passe,* but out in the Victorian Mallee – land of wheat, wool and sky – there are any number of little towns where it's still 1960, and the debutante ball remains an important annual event.

In Rainbow, it's the main fundraising activity of the year for the district netball club, which puts a notice in the local high school newsletter each October inviting upcoming Year 11 girls to take part in the ball held the following April. The debutantes-to-be and their partners start practising well before Christmas, and once school is back in January they devote several hours a week to dancing, dress and etiquette. Rehearsals culminate in an all-afternoon session on the Sunday before the ball, with the girls in full-length petticoats and the boys in jeans, wondering what to do with their hands.

Asked about the significance of such an event, Mrs Joan Harmer, who has helped to train many a crop of debutantes and escorts over the years, said that it represented a major step toward adulthood. "For most of these young people, it's their first big social outing. In preparing for it, they learn a whole range of manners and social customs, and they learn how to dance properly. As far as I'm concerned, if they learn how to waltz they're in good stead wherever they go for the rest of their lives.

"It's also a growing experience. For most of the boys it's their first time in a formal suit, with cummerbund and white gloves and so on, and for the girls it's usually their first time in a gown. At the beginning it's a bit, well . . . embarrassing, I suppose is the word . . . especially for the boys, but in the end they are all very excited about being given the opportunity to act like young ladies and gentlemen."

BILL BACHMAN

Nervous as a roomful of brides, debutantes at the 1991 Rainbow & District Debutante Ball prepare for the biggest entrance of their young lives. Numbers vary from year to year, but 15 girls, all aged 16 or 17, made their debut in '91.

Having emerged from behind the gigantic chiffon fan stage-centre and successfully negotiated the wobbly wooden ramp behind her, Jenelle Christian sets off across the polished hardwood floor of the Rainbow Civic Centre on the reassuring arm of Tony Martin.

Tiffany Wilson and Matthew Abbott offer their respects to Member of Parliament Peter Fisher and his wife Judy. Like most of the debutantes, Tiffany bought her gown, though some girls make their own. Few are ever actually worn again. Wisely, perhaps, the boys invariably hire their outfits for the night.

One of the highlights of the evening is the presentation dancing, where couples show off not only the steps they have learned during months of training, but also, perhaps, a few impromptu maneuvers of their own. Energetically propelled by the music of "The Blenders," in 1991 they performed The Swing Waltz and The Fascination Waltz to a packed house; to conclude the formal part of the evening, the official party and parents then joined in for The Pride of Erin and some progressive barn dancing.

Formal dancing and speeches over and the worst behind her at last, Simone Gregory shares a moment of happy relief with escort Simon Lawes (RIGHT), and poses for a photograph with a couple of girlfriends (BELOW).

Debutante balls are usually a family affair. Depending on numbers, each girl and boy is allocated a table or a quota of seats, and is allowed to invite family and friends.

Admission is $30 for families, $20 for couples, and $15 a single, and includes a sit-down supper. "Onlookers" are also catered for, tickets at the door, $5 a head, and usually fill every bit of floor space not already taken up by tables and dancing debs.

Softdrinks far outnumber beers on the debutantes' tables. Boyfriends – as distinct from escorts – often lurk in the background, emerging from the shadows every now and then for a squeeze or a whispered exchange. Invariably badly dressed, and in need of a haircut, they usually manage to look like dogs on a leash, trailing reluctantly behind their princesses and wishing they were both somewhere else.

Simone Klemm and Scott Cummins are in danger of being swept away during a lull in proceedings. Once the floor is spotless there will be dancing for all, from ruddy-faced dads to kid sisters in hand-me-down dresses. In true country fashion, the night will probably come to a tumultuous close around 1 a.m. with a slightly hysterical rendition of "The Hokey Pokey."

Overheating is not uncommon after a couple of dozen laps around the dance floor, but decorum requires that one always steps outside before loosening one's collar.

THE ROMANCE OF THE SWAG

I came late to sleeping in a swag, but I was an immediate and loudmouthed convert. The smell of canvas is strangely potent and nostalgic to me. I think of tarps I hid under, tents I sheltered in, my first unyielding pair of Levis. So, lying back with the fire flickering at the edge of vision and the sky reeling back like a pianola roll above me, the stars all dots and dits, a music I cannot read or play, I always think of being nine years old and thrilled to bits.

In a swag, the air is bright on your cheeks. You are snug but freer than you would be in the old fart sack you lay twisted in all those school camps ago. If you're a frequent waker like me, you'll see the night in its progression toward the small, slow death of dawn, and the unfamiliar shadows of walls and tents will not frighten you when you drift into wakefulness. You'll see an owl, a bandicoot, a roo in nocturnal passing. You'll feel the first sun on your face, the dew in your hair, and later, down the track, on the tray of some shuddering Toyota, you'll be glad as hell that you have that swag rolled and wadded between your bum and the half-shot suspension.

Every citizen should be issued a swag at birth. Maybe then, in the suburbs, we could go back to sleeping on the verandahs. Well, we could build more verandahs. Alright, I'll shut up, then.

TIM WINTON

JOHN McGAVIN, BULLCATCHING CAMP
EL QUESTRO STATION, WA

The only things upright to greet this Kimberley
dawn are a 50-year-old Studebaker cattle truck
and an elderly boab tree. John McGavin slumbers
on, wrapped in a patriotic swag.

Betraying Australia's convict origins, the word
swag was originally used to describe stolen booty.
Later it came to mean simply a bundle or parcel,
and eventually a couple of rolled blankets,
preferably blue, containing one's personal
belongings. Henry Lawson celebrated this
uniquely Australian form of luggage in a 1907
essay entitled *The Romance of the Swag*. In it, he
describes in great detail how it should be rolled
and carried, and devotes several pages to an
inventory of the contents of a dead tramp's
bedroll, which included one leg of a pair of
trousers, half a waistcoat, a leaky billy can, three
boots of different sizes, a broken saw blade, a
book on etiquette and courtship, and a small
packet of old portraits and letters.

Today, designer swags with sewn-in mosquito
nets and fancy fabrics are rife among urban
cowboys, but in its most correct form, the swag
still consists simply of a thin mattress, perhaps a
small pillow, and either sheets and blankets or a
sleeping bag, all rolled up with a change of clothes
in a fitted canvas cover. To stockmen and other
outback denizens, a good swag is just as important
as a broad hat, a comfortable pair of boots, and a
sensible dog.

(LEFT) BOAB GROVE, PIVOT HILL
EAST KIMBERLEY, WA

Dreamtime figures glow against a spinning sky.
Is it the view from a camp bed, or a scene
projected onto the back of a closed eyelid?

ERICA ELLIOTT, MOROAK STATION • ROPER RIVER, NT

Come November, up in the top end of Australia the nights get a little too warm and breathless for sleeping inside, and all of a sudden the hunt is on for a cool spot to camp. Dogs take up residence beneath the house, or dig in under a big mango tree. Humans move out onto the sleeping porch, set up a stretcher in the garden, or throw a swag down on the handiest bit of concrete they can find – anyplace that cools down fast or catches a bit of breeze is better than a stuffy old bedroom.

The kids' trampoline is Moroak governess Erica Elliott's idea of five-star slumbering. The air circulation's great, it's high enough off the ground to discourage even the most amourous of snakes from crawling in with you, and there's stacks of room to spread right out and wrap your arms around your favourite pillow.

(LEFT) MERV WORTLEY, RUBY PLAINS STATION • WEST TANAMI, WA

Fresh out of the saddle after a long day's mustering, head stockman Merv Wortley catches up with his mail by the light of a gas lantern. Next is dinner, then bed. No TV, no card-playing, no nothing. By 9 o' clock, he'll be stretched out in his swag on that old wire frame, reading the stars.

(RIGHT) CANE GRASS AND STAR TRAILS • INGLIS GAP, WEST KIMBERLEY, WA

DOGS? THEY RUN THE COUNTRY

Dogs? They run the country. I'm sure they sit on numerous shire councils. They are in every family portrait and civic frieze, on car roofs and bike seats.

The Holden ute was built for dogs. The back of the ute is a ship's bridge to a kelpie. He paces, struts, barks directions, offers a blind eye, an unseemly erection, and you are safe from him dribbling slag down the back of your neck, buffered by the glorious and smudged cab window. The farm dog is smarter than many a farmer, kinder than many a bank manager and sweeter smelling than any biker. He can do things that you and I can't, many that we daren't. He is a force to be reckoned with, his own local colour, in a mangy sort of way, but he has the unfortunate habit of licking his reproductive bits before he licks your face, so his evolution is not complete.

TIM WINTON

"CHUCK" AND ROSS THOMPSON • NARDLAH STATION, SOUTHWEST WA

According to a recent survey, in 1992, 37 per cent of Australian households owned one or more dogs. If they'd looked into it a bit further, the researchers might well have concluded that 37 per cent of Australian dogs owned one or more humans, too.

(LEFT) "SPARK" • STRATHAYR STATION, NEAR RICHMOND, TASMANIA

Australia has managed to legislate a lot of the fun out of living in recent years, but at least no one's made helmets compulsory for dogs. Yet.

SPECTACLED DOG • SNAKE CREEK, NORTH QUEENSLAND

SPECKLED DOG • WONGA, NORTH QUEENSLAND

"MAJOR" AND ART MULLER • EL QUESTRO STATION, EAST KIMBERLEY, WA

Ever notice how dogs dominate the space they inhabit . . .

TRAVELLER'S ADVISORY • CLONCURRY, NORTHWEST QLD

. . . whether they're actually there or not?

"CARA" • SWEERS ISLAND, GULF OF CARPENTARIA, QLD

The dog population of Sweers Island, a sandy speck in the South Wellesley Group, is two.

Cara, a Queensland blue heeler with a taste for daredevilry, belongs to Tex and Lyn Battle, who run a small fishing resort.
When not wingwalking, she can often be found riding on the roof of the island's only ute, or decorating the bow of a speeding dinghy.

"CUJO" AND RAY HARDING • SWEERS ISLAND, GULF OF CARPENTARIA, QLD

Cujo, who lives in another camp a bit further along the western shore, is much more safety-conscious.
He prefers guardrails, and wears a seatbelt at all times, even when riding in the back.

RAMBO AND SUZY WONG WITH DON KETTERINGHAM • WOOLEEN STATION, MURCHISON DISTRICT, WA

In a manner of speaking, dogs are the only family some blokes have.

Don Ketteringham's actually got a brother who lives in the district, although he hardly ever sees him.
But then, siblings and dogs aren't in the same category. A man can easily go a year or two
without seeing his brother . . . but a day without dogs is no day at all.

BUTCH, DUTCH, CUJO AND CRAIG HACKETT • KUNUNURRA, EAST KIMBERLEY, WA

Craig Hackett's the same. He's not married, and still lives with his parents, but has three kids who go everywhere with him, and never once ask for an ice cream or say "When are we gonna get there, Dad ?"

TREES AS MEN WALKING

There is a story in the gospel of St Mark of a man healed miraculously of blindness, where in his awe and excitement, as sight comes blurrily to him, he declares that he sees "men as trees, walking." As a child the truth of this beautiful image never left me. I grew up seeing trees that developed almost parallel to the ground in the relentless sou'wester. Their crowns dragged in the dirt, their flaking trunks looked flayed and, seen together, these trees seemed human. I saw them as slaves, a cowed and downtrodden people.

It came as no surprise to hear adults speak of limbs and crowns and scars when speaking of Australian native trees, for they are strangely corporeal. They have such a queer bodily form that quite often their foliage is merely decorative, almost incidental.

On a vast red plain a tree is always a human figure until it declares itself a tree. It takes no imagination to see two entwined boabs as lovers, a group of peeling eucalypts by a farm gate as cow cockies chewing the fat, sun-dried and melancholy. And to see a karri forest is to witness an army, a force beyond reason – to see trees as men walking.

TIM WINTON

TRUNK OF RAINFOREST TREE • LAMINGTON NAT PK, SOUTHEAST QLD

KARRI FOREST NEAR PEMBERTON SOUTHWEST WA

Eucalyptus diversicolor is the tallest tree in Western Australia, and can grow to 85 metres. It is endemic to a relatively small area, from near Albany west to Cape Leeuwin, where the annual rainfall exceeds 1000 mm. It is a true "gum," with smooth bark on a shaft-like trunk. It periodically sheds its old bark to reveal fresh skin in varying patterns of orange, yellow, grey and white – hence its scientific name. The karri forests of the Southwest attract many tourists, and the timber itself is one of Australia's most prized hardwoods.

RIVER RED GUM • FREW RIVER, NT   PALM TREE • GEORGETOWN, QLD

SNAPPY GUM • EAST KIMBERLEY, WA

BOAB TREES • EAST KIMBERLEY, WA

PAINTING AT ABANDONED LEPROSARIUM
DERBY, WEST KIMBERLEY, WA

The bloated belly of the boab tree has appealed to both artists and travellers since the early days of Kimberley exploration. These grotesque inhabitants of the northwest landscape can grow to prodigious size and live to many hundreds of years. On the outskirts of Derby, the huge (some 14 metres across) hollow boab caricatured here was used as the town lock-up during the frontier days of the 1890s.

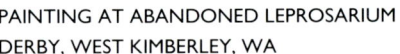

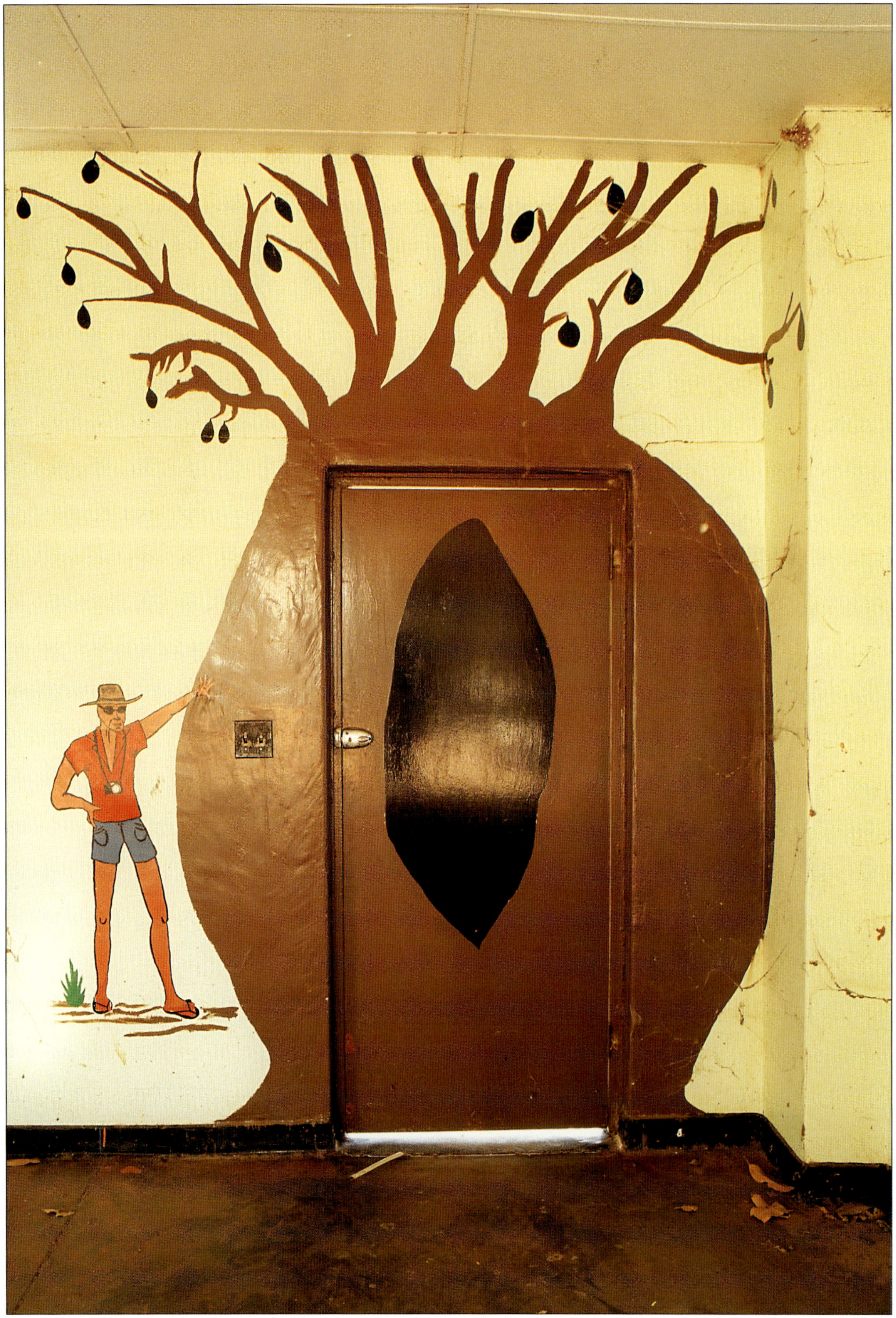

BRITTLE RANGE GUM
LAWN HILL NAT PK, NORTHWEST QLD

Graceful as the boab is ungainly, the candelabra-like brittle range gum grows almost exclusively on rocky outcrops in low to medium rainfall areas across the top end of Australia. Its smooth, sinuous branches contrast with small, rough leaves.

GHOST GUMS, TREPHINA GORGE • EAST MACDONNELL RANGES, NT

Australia is one of the few countries in the world that is associated in the minds of many people with a single plant: the gum tree. "The gum tree," however, is in fact a large and complex genus called *Eucalyptus* that includes more than 500 species, ranging from prostrate dwarfs to some of the largest trees on earth. Within each species, each tree is an individual, sometimes so unlike its neighbours that it might appear to belong to a different order altogether.

The great variety of form and colour displayed by eucalypts have not only been enthusiastically exploited by generations of Australian artists, but have also provoked a gamut of aesthetic responses.

The renowned landscape watercolourist, Hans Heysen, thought the gum tree to be one of nature's wonders:

Its main appeal to me has been its combination of mightiness and delicacy – mighty in its strength of limbs and delicate in the quality of its covering. [As well], I know of no other tree which is more decorative, both as regards the flow of its limbs and the patterns the bark makes on its main trunk. In all its stages the gum tree is extremely beautiful . . .

quoted in William Moore,
THE STORY OF AUSTRALIAN ART (1934)

The English sociologists Beatrice and Sydney Webb, however, who visited Australia in 1898, didn't think much of the gum tree (nor anything else Australian, for that matter):

The gum tree is peculiarly unattractive; not only from its tired colouring but because it seems to have no organic form. [It] likens, more than anything, the attempt of a child to draw a tree, its trunk, branches and twigs spreading themselves in jerky straight lines in every direction with little tufts of feathery foliage at each extremity.

from Beatrice's diary, quoted in AUSTRALIA BROUGHT TO BOOK (Ed. Kay Harman, 1985)

SUGAR GUM • EYRE PENINSULA, SA

LEMON-SCENTED GUM BARK • VICTORIA

RAIN-SOAKED EUCALYPT BARK • NUMINBAH VALLEY, NORTHEAST NSW

SPOTTED GUM BARK • CARNARVON GORGE, QLD CENTRAL HIGHLANDS

PEELING EUCALYPT BARK • CARNARVON GORGE, QLD CENTRAL HIGHLANDS

TREE FERN AND PRECIPICE SANDSTONE • CARNARVON GORGE, QLD CENTRAL HIGHLANDS

Almost as if by design, a tree fern adds a touch of vigour to the petrified pastels along Carnarvon Creek. According to art historian David Hansen (THE FACE OF AUSTRALIA, 1988), in 19th century colonial art it was the green, spreading fern and not the drab, straggly gum tree that was commonly used to symbolise Australia. The use of native flora as a sign of nationality later extended to the wattle and the waratah as well – but overall, the gum tree has always remained the artist's sentimental favourite.

KURRAJONG TREE AND IRONSTONE CLIFF-FACE • HAMERSLEY GORGE, KARIJINI NAT PK, WA

A lone sign of vitality in an exhausted landscape, this kurrajong belongs to a family spread widely around northern Australia. Lace Barks, Flame Trees and Queensland bottle trees are all cousins. A deciduous tree, it is a common inhabitant of rocky slopes, and flowers between October and December.

A mob of mulgas. A gaggle of gum trees. A choir of coolibahs.
Viewed collectively, Australia's trees can sometimes be seen as human figures
in the landscape, lacking only the power of locomotion to bring them alive.

MULGA TREES AND SPRING WILDFLOWERS • EAST PILBARA, WA

RIVER RED GUMS • FORTESCUE FLOODPLAIN, EAST PILBARA, WA

(RIGHT) GUM TREES AND CANE GRASS • EAST KIMBERLEY, WA

THEY'RE RACING AT
AT
FLEMINGTON

The Melbourne Cup is the Australasian National Day. It would be difficult to overstate its importance. It overshadows all other holidays and specialized days of whatever sort in that congeries of colonies. Overshadows them? I might almost say it blots them out. Each of them gets attention, but not everybody's; each of them evokes interest, but not everybody's; each of them rouses enthusiasm, but not everybody's [...but] Cup Day, and Cup Day alone, commands an attention, an interest, and an enthusiasm which are universal – and spontaneous. Cup Day is supreme – it has no rival. I can call to mind no specialized annual day, in any country, which can be named by that large name – Supreme. I can call to mind no specialized annual day, in any country, whose approach fires the whole land with a conflagration of conversation and preparation and anticipation and jubilation. No day save this one; but this one does it.

Mark Twain, FOLLOWING THE EQUATOR (1897)

MELBOURNE CUP FASHION PARADE • PETER'S HOTEL, SPRINGSURE, QLD

MELBOURNE CUP FASHION PARADE • SETTLERS TAVERN, MARGARET RIVER, WA

Cup-Day-Buffet, Peter's Hotel, Springsure, QLD

Although officially a holiday only in the state of Victoria, the first Tuesday in November is fervidly celebrated in many other parts of Australia as well. A hush descends on the entire nation for the three and a half minutes or so that it takes to run the race itself, but rural Australians often devote the whole day to this singular procession of horse flesh. Country race meetings are often held in conjunction with the Cup; pubs and clubs put on luncheons and sweeps and fashion parades; beer cans pop and satellite dishes crackle with incoming signals as people gather in humpies and beach huts and homesteads in the remote corners of the continent. Everywhere you go a great sense of occasion surrounds the event and generates scenes every bit as colourful as those found at Flemington itself.

BILL BACHMAN

MELBOURNE CUP SWEEP • PETER'S HOTEL, SPRINGSURE, QLD

183

(ABOVE) QUEEN'S ARMS HOTEL, SPRINGSURE, QLD

The running of the Melbourne Cup might produce a roomful of suits and fancy hats or a mob of people in shorts and thongs sitting around a telly on an upturned milk crate in the shade of a Moreton Bay fig. The one sure thing is that more Australian TV sets and radios will be switched on at Cup time than at any other moment of the year.

(LEFT) SETTLERS TAVERN, MARGARET RIVER, WA

(BELOW) PETER'S HOTEL, SPRINGSURE, QLD

LIGHT THAT BLINDS, LIGHT THAT BLESSES

Except at dawn and dusk, much of this land is barely visible for light. Illuminated, you might say, within an inch of its life. At midday it drives the eye closed the way flies clamp your teeth shut. The angle of the sun is so uncompromising, the light so white, the shadows so impenetrably black that it seems you are being neutralised, if not completely blinded. The sky is almost colourless, just a waving texture of heatbands.

Sunsets are brilliant and early evening light mellow, but the land feels spent then, simply relieved that the worst is behind it for the day.

The real treat is the dawn, when the country is transformed by a fresh kind of light, and a penetrable, living population of shadows springs up, wherein things shuffle and dip and poise. Birds and animals have voices then. The downstroked leaves of eucalypts have a fresh gloss and there is a kindness, even an optimism in the light.

But, as Randolph Stow writes in his novel *Tourmaline*, "It is not the same country at five in the afternoon. That is the hardest time, when all the heat of the day rises, and every pebble glares, wounding the eyes, shortening the breath; the time when the practice of living is hardest to defend, and nothing seems easier than to cease, to become a stone, hot and still. At five in the afternoon, there is one colour only, and that is brick-red, burning."

TIM WINTON

SNAPPY GUMS, MUNJINA GORGE • KARIJINI NAT PK, WA

LIMPINWOOD VALLEY, NORTHEAST NSW

Early morning, and a tiny settlement awakens in the embrace of verdant hills near Mt Warning.
Although vast landholdings are the norm in Australia, certain parts of the country are suited to farming in a relatively cosy context.
But bucolic splendour rarely comes unaccompanied by a sense of isolation, or perhaps more accurately, an *awareness* of the boundless bush looming
just beyond the home paddock. Always there is the sense of overwhelming sky and space, of nature being greater than man.

Colour depends on light. With it come the riches of the rainbow.
As daylight changes according to the season, the hour, and the natural filtration provided by the atmosphere, so too does colour change.
If you photograph the same scene at two hour intervals starting at six in the morning, you'll get a diverse sequence of photographs, no two alike.
In each image, the colours will be different, the shading will be different, the moods will be different.
And the next day, everything will change again.

(ABOVE) SPRING WILDFLOWERS • EAST PILBARA, WA (LATE AFTERNOON)

(TOP RIGHT) SPEARGRASS SAVANNAH • ROPER RIVER, NT (EARLY AFTERNOON)

(BOTTOM RIGHT) BRITTLE RANGE GUMS • LAWN HILL NAT PK, QLD (TWILIGHT)

BLOODWOOD AND SMOKEBUSH NEAR HALLS CREEK, WA

SPINIFEX-COVERED HILLSIDE NEAR BORROLOOLA, NT

There is an infinity of landscape here, caused by the purity of the atmosphere.
It has been said there is a lack of colour. It is not so obvious as the greenness of England, but it is infinitely more varied and more delicate in tone.
The landscape is a pinky mauve, a lilac, and the reflection of the sun on the particles of the atmosphere is a warm amber.
So I should say our colour scheme is amber and lilac.

Hans Heysen, quoted in William Moore, THE STORY OF AUSTRALIAN ART (1934)

MT SONDER • WEST MACDONNELL RANGES, NT

COASTAL SANDSTONE, GANTHEAUME POINT • BROOME, WA

In Europe the tree forms and the hills are more massed and much more simply composed. Our trees are comparatively thinner in their outlines and the vast spaces emphasize their singular forms . . .

The dominant notes of the colour of the bush, I should say, are bronze, green, ochres, and browns, which give our landscape a lower and more sombre key than in Europe. Ours is called a new country, but what impresses the landscape painter is its extreme oldness and the primitiveness of its quaint forms in trees (and) hills.

Elioth Gruner, quoted in William Moore,
THE STORY OF AUSTRALIAN ART (1934)

(LEFT) ORD RIVER WETLAND, LAKE KUNUNURRA
EAST KIMBERLEY, WA

(RIGHT) RANGELAND NEAR PYRAMID HILL,
MILLSTREAM-CHICHESTER NATIONAL PARK
PILBARA REGION, WA

(GATEFOLD, OVERLEAF) AFTERGLOW ON
MUDSTONE CLIFFS, SWEERS ISLAND
GULF OF CARPENTARIA, QLD

This is the Australian Never-Never, the back of beyond; hard, raw, barren, and blazing. Yet it is not malevolent in appearance. There is something deceptively soft about its water-colour tints of pinks and umbers. It is a subtle desert, insinuating itself into the background of Australian life, even to the life of the factory worker in a southern city or the sports-car enthusiast who never leaves the bitumen. Its presence cannot be forgotten for long by the inhabitants of its fertile fringe. It colours all folk-lore and the borrowed aboriginal mythology . . .

Robin Boyd, THE AUSTRALIAN UGLINESS (1960)

COUNTRY PUB • NORTH BOURKE, NSW

The golden light of late afternoon transforms a simple, shabby facade
into an eyecatching geometry of colour and shadow.

SUNSET AFTERGLOW, KING SOUND • DERBY, WA

Film often sees what the human eye cannot. Here, it reveals local colour
of the sort seldom found on any painter's palette.

LIVING THE LIFE

Why does the sight of a grizzled face beneath a sweat-stained Akubra ring some kind of bell in the heart of the suburban Australian?

Because the people of the outback are the custodians of the national symbols, the keepers of the flame, the dwellers across the time warp. To the majority of coastal consumers these outdoor people are Living the Life and we are living vicariously through them, through literature, art, tourism, and most potently, through advertising.

But it's not just the life of open spaces, of horse and sheep and cattle and campfires and swags unrolled beneath the terrible night sky, not just the life of flood and famine and bushfire – the life our European forebears lived – but also the life *we* lived until ten or fifteen years ago. Out there in their cotton frocks and elastic-sided shorts, among the beetroot stains and Tally-Ho papers, those people are still smoking a pack a day and drinking like there's no tomorrow. They're fanging away at great slabs of red meat and serving tubs of gravy and failing to ingest bales of fibre. They're not guilty about slaughtering animals or scratching the duco. They are not fazed by a rasher of bacon or an aluminium saucepan. A banana prawn is more than a bent and leggy form of cholesterol.

These people do not wear bicycle helmets, or even seatbelts in their cars half the time. They have yet to evolve to the point of power walking or wondering audibly about their toilet training as young meateaters long ago. The tide of fear has not reached them yet. They are so swimmingly . . . unafraid.

Sure, they're dying earlier than we are, and they're more likely to be broke, and no politician will lend them an ear or a buck, but they are still caught sweetly between the Dreaming and the California Dreaming. They're living the life we had before the government health warnings, before we foundered on commonsense.

Yes, they're doing it hard, alright, and it's all the more vivid and heroic, because we can still remember it ourselves. As a nation we still dream of dying with our boots on and our mouths full.

TIM WINTON

MURAL ON SUPERMARKET WALL • KATHERINE, NT
DESIGN © COLIN HOLT 1990

YARDING CATTLE, MAGGIEVILLE OUTSTATION • GULF SAVANNAH NEAR NORMANTON, QLD

Bush diets and lifestyles are not always healthy, with liver disease, skin cancer, emphysema and high cholesterol right up there on the average stockman's list of hazards. But all are pale and distant dangers compared with what gets dished out in the cattleyards when there's a bit of work on. At least there a bloke gets to worry about things he can see.

YARDING CATTLE, ALDERLEY STATION • CHANNEL COUNTRY NEAR BOULIA, QLD

Dust in the wake of 'em: see the wild break of 'em!
Spear-horned and curly, red, spotted and starred:
See the lads bringing 'em, blocking 'em, ringing 'em,
Fetching 'em up to the wings of the yard!

Barcroft H.T. Boake, *Twixt the Wings of the Yard* (1897)

YARDING CATTLE, NAPPERBY STATION • SOUTHEAST TANAMI NEAR ALICE SPRINGS, NT

DANNY TCHOOGA, WILLIAM MANDIJARRA, NELSON SKEEN, BARNEY ROSE AND PETER SKEEN • TANAMI DOWNS, NT

These Aboriginal stockmen have come across the border from Balgo, in the West, to spend a week mustering and branding cattle on Tanami Downs.
New boots, new shirts and clean hats identify some of them as casual contract ringers. After a few days in camp they will probably not look quite so dapper.

BULLDOGGING A YOUNG STEER • TANAMI DOWNS, NT

For some of this crew, however, the romance of being a cowboy fades a bit when there's real work to be done. Head stockman Charlie McAdam and station boss Adam Parbury take the bull by the horns, as it were, with plenty of moral support from the sidelines but precious little hands-on help.

TOYOTA DREAMING • TANAMI DOWNS, NT

Australia lacks some of the unifying symbols that one expects of a developed country. Our flag provokes much dissension, and our national anthem is more dirge than hymn of patriotic joy. Yet there are still images that stir us more than any song or bit of fabric. For some, it's the sight of a western red kangaroo at full stretch, or a big river gum soaring into the sky, or a perfect six-foot wave on a warm summer morning. For others, nothing epitomises Australia more than a stockman, a horse, and a Toyota trayback set against a field of red, white and blue.

CATTLE MUSTER, McARTHUR RIVER STATION • GULF SAVANNAH, NT

This day started before the sun came up and it's been a long ride to a muddy waterhole.
Things like a bogged cow will just have to wait until the horses have had their fill.

ROADSIDE MURAL • MARRABEL, SA

The Australian, one hundred to two hundred years hence, will still live with the consciousness that, if he only goes far enough back over the hills and across the plains, he comes in the end to the mysterious half-desert country where men have to live the lives of strong men. And the life of that mysterious country will affect Australian imagination much as the life of the sea has affected that of the English. It will always be there to help the Australian to form his ideals . . .

C.E.W. Bean, THE DREADNOUGHT OF THE DARLING (1911)

(RIGHT) CHARLIE McADAM, HEAD STOCKMAN • TANAMI DOWNS, NT

Now in his late fifties, Charlie McAdam was born near Halls Creek and grew up at Beagle Bay Mission, north of Broome. He started working with cattle when he was 13, and has travelled all around Australia as a stockman and drover. None of his children followed in his tracks; all are sportsmen, including sons Gilbert and Adrian, both AFL footballers.

NONI BROOME, ALDERLEY STATION
NEAR BOULIA, WESTERN QLD

Noni Broome works alongside three men on a 2600
sq km property that carries 26,000 sheep and 3500
cattle. There is no sexual discrimination or stereotyping.
Basically, whatever the men can do, she can do.

There has always been a great tradition of women on
the land in Australia. Many young, single women are
attracted to the horses, the cattle, the rough anonymity.
Others marry into rural life, and take on a range of
responsibilities that are often greater than those of their
male mates and can include child care, book work and
financial management, community work, education,
ministering to the needs of the local Aborigines, and,
of course, cooking and bottle-washing.

Lately there has also been much talk of an emerging
"feminist consciousness" in various parts of the bush,
where brute development is being replaced with farming
and grazing techniques that actually care for the land.
Even in the diehard bush, where things are slow to
change, there is room for new ways of thinking and doing.

ANGELA MATSON, McARTHUR RIVER STATION
GULF REGION, NT

We first glimpsed Angela Matson emerging from a swim in Bessie Springs, clad in a black lace teddy which accommodated her rather pleasantly. I met her again about an hour later over in the cattle yards, where the 17-year-old jillaroo from Port Lincoln, SA, was helping load cattle bound for Longreach. She had covered the teddy – at least partially – with black tights and a loose, open, white shirt. An Akubra completed The Look. She had complained earlier about the heat, and I ventured that the black tights perhaps didn't help. She justified them as "protective clothing," to which the truck driver, looking on contemplatively from the shade of his rig, added "yeah, against boys."

All things of idyllic seeming in this life are the most difficult – a windjammer, a genius, a beautiful woman, gold. Prose and poetry have glorified the drover's existence into "the vision splendid of the sunlit plains extended." Romance flows in the camp-fire light, and rings in the rhythm of the riding.

It is doubtful whether there is a more arduous calling on earth. Truly it has its poetry, but the men are too weary to find it. In the long hard days, they pay the price of the poet's inspiration. To them the everlasting stars are merely sleepless nights.

Ernestine Hill, *Overlanders* (WALKABOUT, 1940)

Despite a frontier tradition similar to that of the United States, the word *cowboy* never really caught on in Australia. One of the earliest equivalents was *jackeroo*, a term later adapted to *jillaroo* in the case of women. *Rouseabout* and *leatherneck* were both used to refer to station workers of the handyman variety, and the word *ringer* was also coined as a sobriquet for stockmen. (Originally, the term was *ringneck*, referring to the white collars often worn by new arrivals to the bush.)

Today, station hands who work with cattle are called either jackeroos or ringers, depending on what part of the country you're in. Apart from a curvature and gait that have a lot to do with hours spent in the saddle, they have certain other things in common.

For one, they are overworked and underpaid – though they rarely complain about either. They do what they do for reasons other than money, and the hours, and the dirt, and the danger, well . . . they come with the Territory, so to speak.

They are also extremely mobile, even itinerant, one could say. Some, after a spell in the bush, go back to the cities and get real jobs and settle down. Others just keep moving around from station to station, Living the Life, stirring the gene pool, keeping the legend alive.

(CLOCKWISE FROM LEFT)

ROADSIDE MURAL • MARRABEL, SA
NED MCCORD • BAUHINIA DOWNS, NT
DEBBIE ROBERTS • NAPPERBY STATION, NT
JASON TAYLOR • RUBY PLAINS, WA
RICHARD OATES • NAPPERBY STATION, NT
MARTIN ("HARRY") FITZGERALD • NAPPERBY STATION, NT
ALAN HETHERTON • NAPPERBY STATION, NT

A MOTLEY MENAGERIE

It could be the solitude, the madness of the day at the wheel or the night by the fire, but there are times when anything that moves is funny. The emu wants to race, the roo wants to direct traffic. The birds are over-dressed and shrieking like the wives of over-extended tycoons. The ants go sci-fi and the reptiles jauntily suicidal. You don't mind fauna in its place, but the livestock seem to be . . . . . . well, staring.

TIM WINTON

COW IN HAYFIELD NEAR BIRREGURRA • WESTERN DISTRICT, VICTORIA

(RIGHT) CLYDESDALE HORSE, GERALKA STATION • NEAR SPALDING, SA

LAMB IN GRAIN STUBBLE NEAR PARKES, NSW

Over the last 200 years, white settlers have introduced to Australia a variety of non-native animals: cats, horses, camels, foxes, starlings, goats, cattle, rabbits, sheep and cane toads, to name a few. Almost all of them, with their hard hooves and unfriendly habits, have degraded the land and deprived homegrown species of valuable habitats. In environmental terms, even the innocent lamb has a lot to answer for.

AUSTRALIAN BUSTARD IN GRAIN STUBBLE NEAR EMERALD, QLD

Also called Plains Turkeys, these large, aloof-looking birds were once found in open country all over Australia. Flocks numbering in the hundreds were recorded in various inland regions around the turn of the century, but since then the bustard has gradually disappeared from the more closely-settled areas of southern Australia. Alteration of its grassland habitat by grazing, predation by foxes, and widespread illegal shooting have all contributed to this decline. Today, it is found in abundance only in drier parts of the north.

GALAH • EYRE PENINSULA, SA

Distributed throughout most of Australia, galahs are such a common sight that their sartorial charm is often taken for granted. They are voracious birds, usually found in foraging flocks of up to 1000, and are generally detested by graziers and grain growers. During the breeding season they pair off and nest in holes or hollows in trees. Accomplished acrobats and strong fliers, they travel as far as 15 km in the search for food, at speeds up to 50 km/h. On the wing, *en masse*, they form whirling clouds of pink and grey – a thrilling sight above the farming landscapes of the interior.

SPINIFEX PIGEON • HAMERSLEY RANGES, WA

Spinifex pigeons are among the few types of birds to permanently inhabit the arid grasslands of central and northern Australia. The red-bellied variety pictured here occupies the stony ranges of the Western Australian Pilbara. They depend on infrequent rain to replenish waterholes and trigger the seed crops on which they feed. Artful camouflage allows them to blend into the ochre landscape, and they often walk for long distances, normally flying only in short, explosive bursts of 30 metres or less.

PINK COCKATOO • GREAT AUSTRALIAN BIGHT, WA

During his journey to the interior of New South Wales in 1835, Major Sir Thomas Mitchell wrote in glowing terms about this slightly hysterical bird, noted for its elegant plumage, raucous voice, and mischievous behaviour. Irregularly distributed throughout the arid and semi-arid inland regions, "Major Mitchells" are usually found in pairs or small groups, but this individual is part of a large flock based at the Old Eyre Telegraph Station, where the Nullarbor Plain meets the Great Australian Bight.

RAINBOW BEE-EATERS • EAST KIMBERLEY, WA

Huddled together against the morning chill, a quintet of rainbow bee-eaters share a branch at their winter headquarters outside Fitzroy Crossing. Another widespread species, bee-eaters are also strongly communal, flying in groups of 20 or 30 and often roosting in the same small tree. Consummate aerialists, they capture all their food on the wing, eating mainly wasps, bees and other flying insects – as many as 100 on a good day. They take each victim back to a perch, where they batter it and remove the stinger before eating.

(TOP) CARAVAN PARK MURAL • WALPOLE INLET, SOUTHWEST WA
DESIGN © FRED WATSON 1991

COMMUNITY ARTS PROJECT MURAL • BROKEN HILL, NSW
DESIGN © CLARK BARRETT 1984

More than 3000 species of marine and freshwater fish can be found in and around Australia. With a coastline of 12,500 km – more than a third of the Australian total – Western Australia accounts for a vast number of offshore varieties, two dozen of which have been immortalised by retired signpainter Fred Watson on a weatherboard wall not far from the southwestern tip of the continent.

The first known description of a kangaroo is found in the journal of Captain James Cook, in 1770: ". . . *one of the men saw an animal something less than a grey hound, it was of a Mouse Colour very slender made and swift of foot.*"

There are 62 species of kangaroos and their relatives. They are found everywhere in Australia except above the snowline, and range in size from mouse-like to monstrous. Some live in treetops, while others excavate complex burrows. They are the only large mammal to propel themselves by hopping, and though they normally get along at 10-12 km/h, if pursued they can travel at speeds in excess of 60 km/h.

CROCODILE ATTACK • CABLE BEACH, BROOME, WA

CUT - PRICE MIRACLES

The desert is a nightmare, a vast abstraction, a place of spirits. A good place to survive, perhaps. Something to have witnessed. A pilgrim's place, somewhere to have visions, and more often to die. To those who have belonged, the desert is a spiritual fact, but for the newcomer, a place without people is a problem. So far from the reassurance of the shop and the club, the shimmering indifferent plain is both a proof of a Divine presence and a suggestion of its absence. One moment you are comforted, the next terrified. Perhaps the desert is the great metaphor for God; it is always beyond the idea we have in mind for it. In the Outback, religion in its many forms is both certain and ambivalent, practical and mysterious, dismissed and never understood. Out here, any old bore is an oasis, a cut-price miracle.

TIM WINTON

SPINIFEX ON STONY PLAIN NEAR BALGO HILLS • WEST TANAMI, WA

The strange, as it were, invisible beauty of Australia, which is undeniably there, but which seems to lurk just beyond the range of our white vision. You feel you can't see — as if your eyes hadn't the vision in them to correspond with the outside landscape. For the landscape is so unimpressive, like a face with little or no features, a dark face. It is so aboriginal, out of our ken, and it hangs back so aloof.

D.H. Lawrence, KANGAROO (1923)

TIDAL CREEKS NEAR DERBY • WEST KIMBERLEY, WA

WARLPIRI WOMEN DANCING • LAJAMANU, NORTH TANAMI, NT

No matter how modern the occasion – in this case, a football carnival – the underlying rituals of the Aboriginal way of life are never far from centre stage. Ceremonial dances, which are passed on from one generation to the next, help to preserve and celebrate tribal culture. The painting on the body of this desert woman is called *yawulyu*, and consists of highly personalised totemic designs inherited from mother and father. Traditionally, ochre was used to mark skin primed with emu fat, but today vegetable oil or butter is more commonly used.

For Australia's Aboriginal people, the land is the ultimate reality. Nature *is* life, and not just set-dressing. It lies at the core of their material and spiritual culture, and is the inspiration for almost all of their art. Whereas much of our white European landscape painting *describes* the environment in more or less traditional ways, the Aboriginal equivalent is almost always conceptual, timeless and diagrammatic. On one level, their paintings contain stories rooted in Dreamtime mythology. On others, they are stylised navigational aids to food sources, or spiritual maps pertaining to sacred sites, and sometimes even dispense moral guidance and entertainment. Always, they express the imprint of the land on the native psyche.

WILLIE GUDIPI • SOUTHEAST ARNHEM LAND, NT

Inside his house in the remote Roper River community of Ngukurr, Alawa tribal elder Willie Gudipi displays a painting in progress. The material sparseness of many Aborigines' domestic surroundings contrasts dramatically with the spiritual richness of their art.

PAINTING © WILLIE GUDIPI 1990

KANGAROO/DINGO DREAMING • NAPPERBY STATION, NT

Anmatyere artist Morris Wako holds a canvas which tells the story of a Jambijimba / Jungala tribal dreaming associated with country to the west of Yuendemu. The central panel represents sandhills, and the outer concentric circles are waterholes connected by underground channels. The dingo and kangaroo are shown travelling in opposite directions along the watercourse.

PAINTING © MORRIS WAKO 1992

CHURCH INTERIOR, MARBLE BAR • EAST PILBARA, WA

The golden light of morning sanctifies an abandoned Catholic church
desecrated by vandals in a remote northwest mining town.

LEICHARDT RIVER • GULF SAVANNAH, NORTHWEST QLD

Like a divine compass, an enigmatic signpost offers encouragement to pilgrims
on the road from Burketown to Normanton.

229

MULTIPLE-CHOICE SHOPFRONT • CLONCURRY, NORTHWEST QLD

GAVIN COWLAN, DOCTORS CREEK • NEAR DERBY, WEST KIMBERLEY, WA

Fisher of men or just plain fisherman? Twenty-seven-year-old Gavin Cowlan will tell you
he's certainly no Bush Messiah, but his words evoke the alienation that pervades much of rural Australia:
"The real Australia? It's the cities, mate, for sure. That's what Australia's all about these days. We're all forgotten
people out here. At times it's like we don't even exist, or at least don't belong to Australia."

Three well-known writers – a foreign visitor, an English-born naturalist
who emigrated to Australia in 1839, and an experienced bushman –
present contrasting views on The Great Australian Emptiness.

CATTLE AT BORE • CHANNEL COUNTRY NEAR BOULIA, WESTERN QLD

Driving through those enormous stretches of flat pasture land, with nothing to break the horizon except periodic windmills,
I realised how frightening it could be: how easy to get lost – ' bushed ' – as the saying was.
The sun was so high over your head that you had no idea of north, south, east or west.

Agatha Christie, 1922, from her autobiography

ABANDONED HUT NEAR MARREE, SA

In England we plant groves and woods, and think our country residences unfinished and incomplete without them;
but here the exact contrary is the case, and unless a settler can see an expanse of bare, naked, unvaried, shadeless, dry dusty land
spread all around him, he fancies his dwelling 'wild and uncivilized.'

Louisa Ann Meredith, NOTES AND SKETCHES OF NEW SOUTH WALES (1844)

BRAHMAN BULL • BARKLY TABLELAND, NT

The sun-bleached plain stretched unbroken to the mirage along the skyline . . .
Some people are distressed by these vast and open landscapes; they feel lost and helpless without familiar landmarks all around them.
But for many the sense of freedom that comes with the sight of a far-off horizon on every side can never be found where neat suburban houses huddle together.

George Farwell, VANISHING AUSTRALIANS (1961)

THE ENDLESS CYCLE

In rural Australia (the old kingdom of Bust and Boom) death is a constant. The land is ravaged by nature as often as serviced by it, and natural disasters are timestrokes people measure their lives by (the Flood of '46, the Fire of '59, the Drought of, the Cyclone of). But in landscape cataclysm can be seen past. The bush recovers from fire by sheer profusion; floods slough off to leave a rare wallpaper of desert flowers. The mechanics of resurrection are always there.

Station kids are matter-of-fact about death. To them there will always be slaughter before food. There will be other cows, more sheep, more roos. They will see them born, and they'll learn the unsentimental ways of their elders. Even pets who live in a special zone of sentiment will die and be buried and replaced. Life and death are the same procession. New things come.

But the ute with the coffin poking out onto the tailgate offers less hope. Human loss is always unmitigated. Rural Australians are stoical, but they give death its due. The antiseptic niceties of the crematorium are not so common here. Whole communities still mourn their dead with wakes and processions. They talk in generations as a way of seeing life and death as the procession they know in the rest of nature, but only the rare believers and the still rarer optimists talk of resurrection out here any more.

TIM WINTON

LARGE GREEN PUSSYTAILS AND TERMITE MOUND · RABBIT FLAT, NT

TERMITE MOUNDS ON BLACKSOIL PLAINS • BARKLY TABLELAND, NT

A cemetery of living headstones covers parched rangeland north of Brunette Downs.
In an arena where primal forces rule, the sun blesses and damns, but only rain brings resurrection.
When it comes, the resulting glory is seldom more than short-lived.

Water water everywhere: in tropical northern Australia the annual monsoon brings new life to vast areas of savannah grassland. Far to the south, near the geographical centre of the continent, an island of sand lies marooned in an ocean of salt.

FLOODPLAIN IN LATE WET SEASON • WESTERN ARNHEM LAND

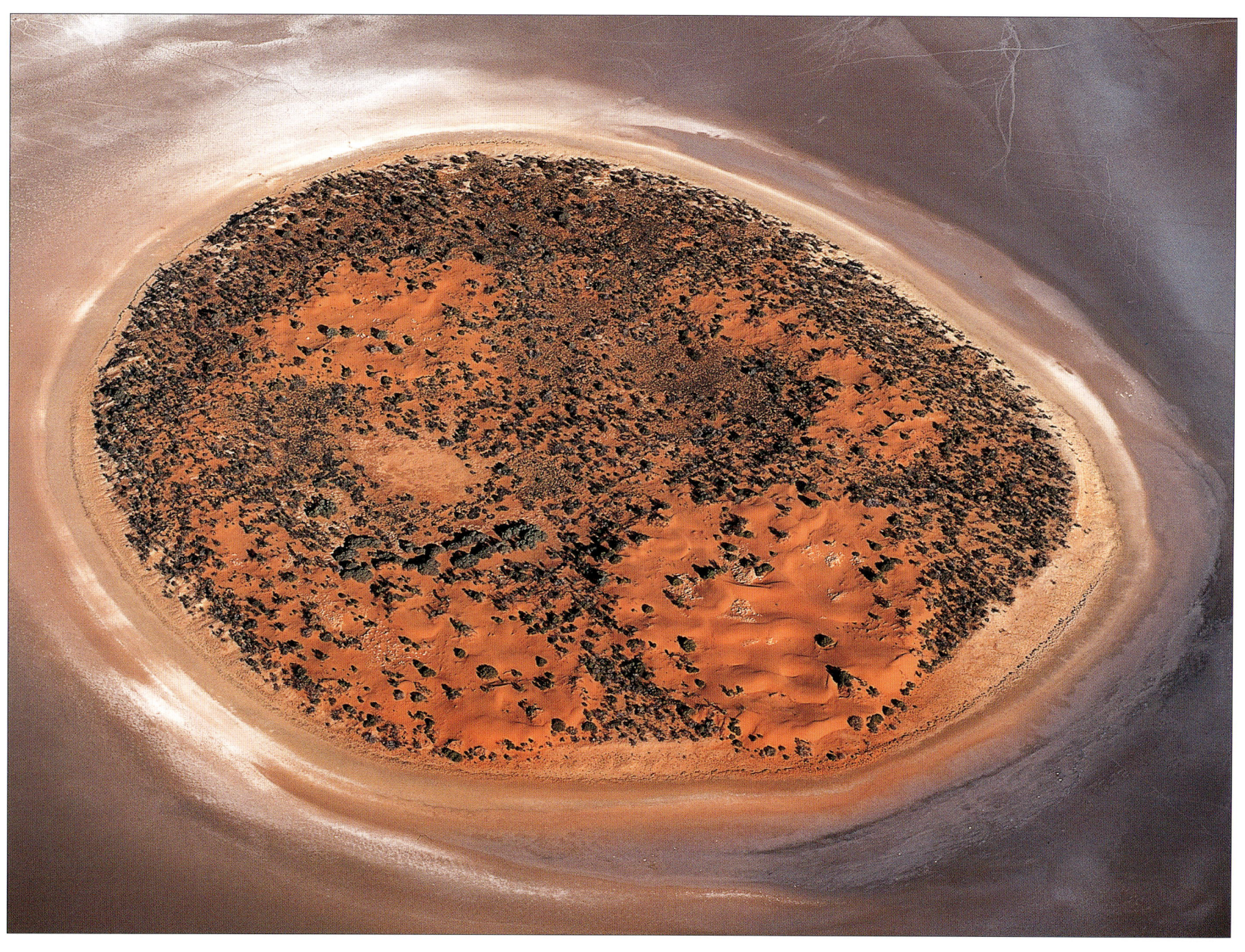

ISLAND IN LAKE AMADEUS • CENTRAL AUSTRALIA

COASTAL DUNES AFTER BUSHFIRE • COFFIN BAY NAT PK, SA

Life follows death in the endless cycle of the bush. In the southwest corner of the Eyre Peninsula, denuded dunes slowly recover from a fierce conflagration. At virtually the same latitude some 1800 km to the west, grass trees and native grasses prosper where, a year previously, a similar blaze triggered seed germination in dunes near Point D'Entrecasteaux.

BUSHFIRE REGROWTH • POINT D'ENTRECASTEAUX, SOUTHWEST WA

There is seldom any dignity to death in the bush. Things come and things go, and their corpses litter the countryside, unmoved and unmentioned. Simple as that. But it's touching all the same to see wildflowers encircling a dead beast's final resting place, and a shaft of golden light bathing a mummified fox, providing an accidental moment of honour to the fallen.

COW CARCASS • ROY HILL STATION, EAST PILBARA, WA

FOX CARCASS IN WOOLSHED • MIDDLEBACK STATION, EYRE PENINSULA, SA

DYING COW • MOROAK STATION, ROPER RIVER, NT

Vital signs are fading fast as an old mate pays his last respects to a dying Brahman cow,
while five-year-old Joey MacFarlane looks impassively on from a ringside seat.

SLAUGHTERING A SHEEP
MIDDLEBACK STATION, EYRE PENINSULA, SA

Traditional station philosophy says that nothing should go to waste. In an offbeat observance of that notion, Andrew Nicolson cuts up a sheep for a weekend barbecue, while daughters Madeleine (in the pink dress) and Lucy sail gum-leaf boats down the river of warm blood.

CEMETERY AT DERBY LEPROSARIUM • WEST KIMBERLEY, WA

Opened in 1936 to help stop the spread of the disease among Aborigines in the
Kimberley region, the leprosarium was once a thriving, self-contained community,
housing a mixed population. It was closed in 1986, and is being redeveloped as an
Aboriginal learning centre. Now overgrown with cane grass, the cemetery contains
hundreds of unmarked graves.

(LEFT) OLD CEMETERY • MARBLE BAR, EAST PILBARA, WA

Certain graves in the old cemetery at Marble Bar are decorated with heavy iron
chains, marking the burial sites of Afghan camel drivers who used to cart wool,
mining supplies and other stores in the area. The chains were part of the harnesses
used on the camel trains. In this photograph, a tree growing on an old gravesite
has enfolded and carried one such chain a short distance skyward.

Content defies context, as flowers spring from a stony plain.
It is on the fringes of the most inhospitable land where one often finds the most beautiful and extraordinary things.

TINY PURSLANE (PARAKEELYA) • TANAMI DESERT, NT

At the edges of pans of clay, where the topsoil has eroded, live waxy succulents bearing bright pink and purple blooms,
spread like splashes of paint dropped in widening circles on the earth.

Jill Ker Conway, THE ROAD TO COORAIN (1989)

MARY WATSON AT ERRABIDDY OUTSTATION
WOOLEEN, MURCHISON DISTRICT, WA

Mary Watson was born in 1903 and grew up in Midland Junction, a suburb of Perth. One of a family of 12, she had never been away from home until she got married at 18 to a fellow who at the time was the station cook at Wooleen, a large sheep station up in the Murchison. James, the husband, told her she'd need a good hat where they were going, but that's about all the information she was given until arriving at Wooleen, which was . . . well, not Midland Junction.

James and Mary were soon sent out to a lonely outstation about 30 kms from the homestead, where they were to live for the next two years. During that time, native girls were Mary's only regular companions, and she went through one 12-month period where she never saw another white woman. While there, she gave birth to two sons. The second died in infancy and was buried in a sandhill near the homestead.

Because of complications resulting from the birth, Mary left Wooleen after losing the baby, and never actually saw his burial site. She eventually had seven children, and for many years worked alongside her husband as a railway employee at various locations around the state. At one time, she was the only station mistress in Western Australia.

In October 1991, at the age of 88, Mary returned to Wooleen after an absence of more than 65 years, in order to find the grave of her infant son, and visit the outstation she'd once lived in.

She is pictured here at the site of the old hut, which was pulled down for materials in 1960. The kurrajong trees in the background grew from seeds planted by her husband in the early 1920s.

"I really missed the place after I left," she told me. "It's wonderful to come back. I never expected to find anything from my past still remaining."

EPILOGUE

BOAB TREE AND TERMITE MOUND NEAR DERBY, WA

And the sun sank again on the grand Australian bush —
the nurse and tutor of eccentric minds, the home of the weird,
and of much that is different from things in other lands.

Henry Lawson, *The Bush Undertaker*
SHORT STORIES IN PROSE AND VERSE (1894)

The author thanks the following individuals and organisations for permission to reproduce copyrighted material in LOCAL COLOUR:

Page 6: Lyric from *The Heartland* by Mike McClellan © The McClellan Consultancy Pty Ltd 1989
Page 51: Community mural, Coles Supermarket, Alice Springs - Design by Bob and Kaye Kessing © The Araluen Centre for Arts and Entertainment
Page 85: Painting *Blood from Stone* © Helen Norton 1991, by permission of the artist
Page 127: Photograph of Aboriginal girl © AUSTRALIAN GEOGRAPHIC 1993
Page 227: Painting *Gabal Ritual* © Willie Gudipi 1990, by permission of Alcaston House Gallery, Melbourne
Page 227: Painting *Kangaroo/Dingo Dreaming* © Morris Wako 1992, by permission of Napperby Artists, via Alice Springs, NT

READING LIST

The following books were the source of many of the quotations appearing in LOCAL COLOUR:

THE DICTIONARY OF AUSTRALIAN QUOTATIONS
edited by Stephen Murray-Smith (Heinemann Publishers, 1984)

AUSTRALIA BROUGHT TO BOOK: RESPONSES TO AUSTRALIA BY VISITING
WRITERS, 1836-1939, compiled and edited by Kaye Harman (Boobook Publications, 1985)

Other important sources of information, ideas and inspiration were, in no particular order:

THE AUSTRALIANS
Robert B. Goodman and George Johnston (Rigby Ltd, 1966)

READER'S DIGEST ILLUSTRATED GUIDE TO AUSTRALIAN PLACES
Reader's Digest (Australia) Pty Ltd, 1993

THE FACE OF AUSTRALIA: THE LAND & THE PEOPLE • THE PAST & THE PRESENT
David Hansen (Australian Bicentennial Authority, 1988)

THE VOYAGE OF THE GREAT SOUTHERN ARK
Reg and Maggie Morrison (Lansdowne Press, 1988)

VANISHING AUSTRALIANS
George Farwell (Rigby Ltd, 1961)

AUSTRALIAN LANDSCAPES
George Farwell (Walkabout Pocketbooks, 1969)

THE OUTSIDE TRACK
George Farwell (Melbourne University Press, 1951)

THE AUSTRALIAN LEGEND
Russel Ward (Oxford University Press, 1965)

THE AUSTRALIAN UGLINESS
Robin Boyd (Penguin Books, 1963)

THE AUSTRALIAN LANGUAGE
Sidney J. Baker (Angus & Robertson, 1945)

WALKABOUT'S AUSTRALIA
ed. A.T. Bolton (Walkabout Pocketbooks, 1968)

THERE'S A TRACK WINDING BACK: REDISCOVERING AUSTRALIA
Phil Jarratt (Pan Macmillan, 1990)

ONE FOR THE ROAD
Tony Horwitz (Harper & Row, 1987)

ROAD TO THE MURCHISON: AN ILLUSTRATED STORY
OF THE DISTRICT AND ITS PEOPLE
Marion Nixon and R.F.B. LeFroy (Shire of Murchison)

LIFE IN AUSTRALIA
ed. Craig McGregor and David Beal (Southern Cross International, 1968)

OUTBACK
Thomas Keneally (Coronet, 1984)

MY AUSTRALIA
Hal Missingham (Collins, 1969)

NORTH OF THE 26TH: WRITINGS, PAINTINGS,
DRAWINGS, AND PHOTOGRAPHS FROM
THE KIMBERLEY, PILBARA AND GASCOYNE REGIONS
ed. Helen Weller (Reeve Books, 1989)

AUSTRALIAN WALKABOUT
ed. Brian McArdle and Peter Fenton (Lansdowne, 1968)

AUSTRALIA AS HUMAN SETTING
ed. Amos Rapoport (Angus & Robertson, 1972)

JOURNEY AMONG MEN
Jock Marshall and Russell Drysdale (Hodder & Stoughton, 1962)

KIMBERLEY: DREAMING TO DIAMONDS
Hugh Edwards, 1991

THE ROAD FROM COORAIN: AN AUSTRALIAN MEMOIR
Jill Ker Conway (Mandarin, 1990)

Bush Culture, THE BULLETIN
January 26/February 2, 1993 (Australia Day Special Edition)

The Great Empty, CONDE NAST TRAVELER
September 1990

PLANTS OF THE KIMBERLEY REGION OF WESTERN AUSTRALIA
R.J. Petheram and B. Kok (University of Western Australia Press, 1983)

READER'S DIGEST COMPLETE BOOK OF AUSTRALIAN BIRDS
(Reader's Digest, 1986)

KEY GUIDE TO AUSTRALIAN TREES
Leonard Cronin (Reed Books, 1988)

THE CENTRE: THE NATURAL HISTORY OF AUSTRALIA'S DESERT REGIONS
Penny van Oosterzee (Reed Books, 1991)

A FIELD GUIDE TO AUSTRALIAN TREES
Ivan Holliday and Ron Hill (Rigby, 1984)

WILDFLOWERS & PLANTS OF CENTRAL AUSTRALIA
Anne Urban (Southbank Editions, 1990)

ACKNOWLEDGMENTS

I am constantly amazed by the exquisite detail contained in a colour slide, and the fact that I actually have such a means to express and record my own way of seeing the world. No less remarkable is the ability of camera and film to consistently produce such perfection, roll after roll, year after year.

When it comes to the cameras themselves, this is partly due to ingenious design and construction, and partly due to first-class professional servicing. It's stupid to pretend that things don't break down or go wrong from time to time. They do, and throughout my travels, they did. But I can honestly say that whenever I had problems with my equipment, it was repaired and returned to me within days, no matter how far away and hard to find I happened to be.

Immeasurable thanks, therefore, to Richard Broadbent, Marco Zeilinger and all the staff in the Photographic Service Division at Canon Australia's Melbourne office. The boys there can even fix things by remote control, as I discovered one day when, faced with a sticky shutter, I rang Marco on my Flying Doctor Radio from the middle of the Tanami Desert. "OK, you see that little lever beside the mirror?" he began. Well, it was a bit like delivering a baby by telephone, but I did what he told me, and it worked.

Thanks also to Bob Pattie at Rudolph Gunz (Photographic) Pty Ltd, for looking after my Bronica and Widelux gear when it got sick.

I owe much gratitude to Paul Thompson, National Marketing Manager for Fuji professional photographic products at Hanimex Pty Ltd, for his belief in this project and his ongoing support throughout. Similarly, thanks to Gordon Graham and Mel Forbes at Kodak Australasia, and Norbert Herrmann at Agfa-Gevaert.

For faithfully and flawlessly processing my film, kudos to Latrobe Colourlab and The Colour Factory (both in Melbourne), and to the Skyroad Express air courier network, for carting it all around the country without ever losing a single roll.

For assistance during the production of LOCAL COLOUR itself, many thanks to Mark Thomson and the staff at Bond Colour Laboratories in Melbourne.

For offering me the opportunity to go places I might not have visited otherwise, thanks to Howard Whelan and Tony Gordon at *Australian Geographic* Magazine and to Tom Duggan, editor of *Qantas Airways* Magazine from 1988 to 1993.

For looking after house and business during our many long absences, love and thanks to Jacqui Mott (1987) and Leanne Temme and Ian McDonald (1990/1991). For dog-sitting (well, *someone* had to stay home), Jacqui again, plus Christine and Rob Sewell, and Andy, Suzy, John and Chris Speirs.

For putting a roof over our heads and temporarily offering a semblance of "normal life" when it came time to edit film, many thanks to Di and Daphne Calder (Alice Springs), David Thomae (Cairns), Ian Crimp (Derby), Phil and Jackie Jarratt (Cooroy), and Lyn and Richard Woldendorp (Perth).

To me, LOCAL COLOUR is not so much a collection of pictures as it is of experiences. Fortunately I had someone to share them with, in the form of my wife, Sally. As travelling companion, business partner, friend and fellow tyre-changer, she contributed to this book in a great many ways. Her keen eye for picture possibilities, her easy way with people, her love of the land, her incredible patience (*never* travel with a photographer, she will tell you if prompted) and adaptability, and her skill with a camp oven and limited groceries are only a few of her many fine qualities. Frankly, I'd travel anywhere with her. Whether the opposite is true remains to be seen.

Finally, I'd like to note that everything they say about the kindness of strangers is true. During our travels we met people too numerous to name who helped us out of various sticky situations, who took us into their lives for a few hours, a day, even a week or two, and who more often than not allowed me to record them and parts of their world on film. All we really had to offer in exchange was our company, a bit of a hand in the kitchen or out in the paddock, and perhaps a few snapshots sent back from further down the track - but I honestly can't remember anyone ever asking us for more.

Happily, some of these farflung people have actually become friends, or at least pen-friends, and many others visit us all the time in my pictures and diaries. It's nice to remember them as often as we do. Without them our travels would have been much less interesting, and this book certainly wouldn't have been possible.

BILL BACHMAN

EQUIPMENT NOTES

"Do you develop your own film?" is by far the most common question that people ask when they find out I am a photographer. Now, frankly, I've never understood why this would even occur to anyone. To be fair, I suppose there are people who actually think that photographers still travel with a black velvet tent and a boxful of chemicals like they used to in the 1870s. God knows we travel with just about everything else.

But the connection between a photographer and his cameras is a vital one, rather like that between a stockman and his horse – both eventually become an extension of one's body. So you can be sure he cares deeply about his own gear, even if he doesn't like talking about it. That pretty well describes me, so I usually just answer the question and then try to find a polite way of changing the subject.

A reliable vehicle is also vital to the success of any long-range photographic expedition . . .

. . . although alternative forms of transport do exist.

A solid tripod is especially useful when using long lenses or photographing small subjects up close. Or both.

Anyway, the answer to that question is "No." The second most common query is "What kind of camera do you use?" Many photographers brush this enquiry aside as if it were of no importance. But I'll let you in on a secret. Any professional who tells you he isn't interested in his camera equipment is lying. He may not be interested in what *anyone else* uses, nor in fact know much about photographic hardware in general.

I have used Canon 35mm cameras and lenses for fifteen years. Between 1987 and 1995 my travelling kit consisted of three T90 bodies (one fitted with a programmable Command Back that enabled me to make long night-time exposures without having to get up at 3AM and stub my toe on the tripod while trying to manually close the shutter) and Canon FD lenses ranging from 17 to 500 mm.

253

First introduced in 1986, the T90 is no longer manufactured, having been superseded by Canon's EOS autofocus series. It was, however, one of the best non-autofocus SLR cameras ever made, and served me well over the years. It was compact, rugged and easy to use, with a fast built-in motor drive – all important features out in the field. I could easily fit one body, four lenses and a light meter in a small waist pack, leaving my hands free for climbing windmills, hanging on in the back of speeding utes, and all the other stupid things photographers do.

In 1995 I switched over to EOS technology, and all of the more recent images in this 1998 edition were taken using this system. But I've still got one T90 and a few FD lenses in my cupboard, just in case....

Keeping fit is also essential while travelling. Mixed aerobics is just one of many fun-filled open-air ways of doing so.

My current camera is the ETRsi, with 40, 50, 75 and 150 mm Zenzanon lenses, and both 6 x 4.5 cm 120 and 35mm panoramic film backs.

This is one of the lightest, simplest medium-format systems available, and one of the few to offer a panoramic option, which I use all the time. I can comfortably carry the whole lot, including four 120 magazines and lots of film, for reasonably long distances in a specially-partitioned backpack. This, the 35mm waist pack described above, and a tripod over one shoulder, comprises my basic "walking-around" kit.

I also have an Art Panorama camera with a Nikkor 90mm f4.5 lens. This uses 120 film and gives six 6 x 12 cm exposures or four 6 x 17 cm exposures per roll. Heavy and rather cumbersome, it is definitely a tripod-only camera, but the results justify the trouble.

For much quicker ultrawide panoramic work, I use a 35 mm Widelux camera, which has a 140-degree angle of view.

Probably the most indispensable piece of equipment for any travelling photographer is a good tripod. Mine is a Manfrotto model 055 with a Cambo CBH3 ball head and a Kirk quick-release clamp. All of my camera bodies are fitted with quick-release plates, which saves a lot of time if you use a tripod as much as I do.

Using a tripod not only gives you a much better chance of having sharp pictures, especially with longer lenses and medium-format cameras; it also induces a more deliberate mood, and makes you think about what you're photographing, not to mention how and why.

Equally important is someplace useful to put said tripod. There were plenty of times when the closest thing to a hill for miles around was my Toyota LandCruiser, so I was frequently grateful for having fitted it with a heavy steel roofrack lined with an 8-ply wooden deck from which I could actually get a drop on the landscape, rather in the manner of a gunner in his turret.

Some of the images in LOCAL COLOUR were made on Kodak and Agfa professional transparency films, but for the vast majority I used Fujichrome Professional in both 35mm and 120 sizes. On the road I normally run one T90 with Fujichrome RDP100 and one with Fuji RVP 50 (Velvia), and keep one camera body spare. Similarly, I generally keep Fuji 100 in one ETR 120-back and Velvia in another, with one back spare, and Velvia in the panoramic back.

Fuji Velvia is incredibly sharp, and delivers warm, vivid colours. Rated at 40 ISO, it is my first choice for landscapes and other outdoor subject matter. For portraits, and to cope with movement or low light, I prefer Fujichrome 100.

Because The Unexpected is regularly encountered in the Outback, a certain amount of flexibility should be built into one's itinerary.

Staying in touch is important when away from the office for months at a time.

Whenever possible, I like to work in a format slightly larger than 35mm for landscapes and other outdoor subject matter with a lot of detail. I have used Bronica's ETR system, which features terrific optics and a variety of interchangeable film backs, since the mid-1970s.

Home, home on the road. It can be a kitchen stove or a campfire, a swag or a double mattress with all the trimmings, a roof over your head or just a net to keep the bugs out. When it comes right down to it, all you really need is a decent light to read by once the sun's gone down.

Virtually all of the colours in this book are exactly as the film saw them. The only filters used were a polarizer, which intensifies but does not change colours, and, occasionally, an 81A filter, which has a slight warming effect.

Carting all this paraphernalia around the country presents numerous challenges, not the least being how to fit it all in one's vehicle and still leave room for self, wife, and incidentals like food, water, bedding and things to read.

We solved the latter by buying a camper-trailer, which left lots of car-space for photographic equipment. On a platform where the back seat would normally be I kept all my camera gear and a 40-litre 12-volt Engel fridge which was mostly reserved for film, usually several hundred rolls at a time. I hung my tripod behind the front seat, suspended from two octopus straps looped around the headrests.

Rather than using hard aluminium cases, which are dustproof − a plus − but are also heavy and have square corners − which makes them hard to pack − I used a variety of soft bags and rucksacks.

Dustproofing was partly prevention (keeping the windows closed and the bags zipped) and partly cure, in the form of a 1.3 cubic metre cylinder of compressed air I somehow managed to find space for. Every couple of weeks when there was a good cross-wind blowing, I would open all the doors and blast everything − cameras, seat covers, car interior, tape deck − you name it, it got the treatment.

I normally shot for four to six weeks between edits, accumulating anywhere between 100 and 300 rolls of film before shipping it all to Melbourne for processing. Consequently one of my biggest anxieties was waiting for the film to come back, and wondering whether everything would "come out okay," as they say. Amazingly, it always did − no camera problems that I didn't already know about, no bad processing, no lost film. The only disappointments were due to mistakes for which I had only myself to blame.

For editing, we carried a small light box, a laptop computer and printer which we used to produce caption labels, and a few basic reference books. It was terribly exciting to see all the new shots but, in the end, editing was a tedious process that lasted anywhere from four days to two weeks, and by the end of these sessions we were almost screaming with impatience to get back on the road. The alternative, however − coming home after nine months to six or eight hundred boxes of unopened slides − was unthinkable. Ritual suicide, and not this book, would probably have been the result.

BILL BACHMAN

Editing slides can be very tiring, and it's important to rest after long sessions at the lightbox.

POSTSCRIPT

I could just as well have called this book SCRATCHING THE SURFACE,
because that's pretty much what it does. In fact, that's pretty much *all* it does.

A few of the photographs date back more than ten years, but most were taken over
a five-year period between 1987 and 1991. About 20 new images,
all taken between 1993 and 1998, are included in this edition.

Over the past decade, on three major trips of more than seven months each and numerous shorter
ones ranging from one to six weeks, I've travelled well over 100,000 kilometres, shot over 1500
rolls of film, and had more than 30 flat tyres. Impressive as those figures may be, whenever I look at
the large map of Australia on which I've marked my travels in different colours, the first thing I see
are the places where I haven't been. Admittedly, some of them are trackless deserts,
but the fact remains: in all my wanderings, I've only just begun to see Australia.

BILL BACHMAN

Since 1992 I've clocked up thousands of additional kilometres, changed a few more tyres,
and drawn quite a few new lines on that map – which is starting to show its age
(along with my LandCruiser). But the big blank spaces are as big as ever. Clearly,
many more photographs – and the experiences that go with them – await.